Biography Today

Profiles of People of Interest to Young Readers

Scientists & Inventors Series

Volume 2
1997

Laurie Lanzen Harris
Executive Editor

Cherie D. Abbey
Associate Editor

Omnigraphics, Inc.

Penobscot Building
Detroit, Michigan 48226

Laurie Lanzen Harris, *Executive Editor*
Cherie D. Abbey, *Associate Editor*
Kevin Hillstrom, Laurie Hillstrom, Sue Ellen Thompson,
and John Wukovitz, *Sketch Writers*
Barry Puckett, *Research Associate*

Omnigraphics, Inc.

* * *

Matt Barbour, *Production Manager*
Laurie Lanzen Harris, *Vice President, Editorial Director*
Peter E. Ruffner, *Vice President, Administration*
James A. Sellgren, *Vice President, Operations and Finance*
Jane Steele, *Marketing Consultant*

* * *

Frederick G. Ruffner, Jr., Publisher

Contents

Preface

Welcome to the second volume of the **Biography Today Scientists and Inventors Series**. We are publishing this new series in response to the growing number of suggestions from our readers, who want more coverage of more people in *Biography Today*. Over the past few years, we have published several special subject volumes, covering **Artists, Authors, Scientists and Inventors, Sports Figures,** and **World Leaders.** Each of these hardcover volumes is 200 pages in length and covers approximately 15 individuals of interest to readers aged 9 and above. The length and format of the entries is like those found in the regular issues of *Biography Today*, but there is **no duplication** between the regular series and the special subject volumes.

The Plan of the Work

As with the regular issues of *Biography Today*, this special subject volume on **Scientists and Inventors** was especially created to appeal to young readers in a format they can enjoy reading and readily understand. Each volume contains alphabetically arranged sketches. Each entry provides at least one picture of the individual profiled, and bold-faced rubrics lead the reader to information on birth, youth, early memories, education, first jobs, marriage and family, career highlights, memorable experiences, hobbies, and honors and awards. Each of the entries ends with a list of easily accessible sources designed to lead the student to further reading on the individual and a current address. Obituary entries are also included, written to provide a perspective on the individual's entire career. Obituaries are clearly marked in both the table of contents and at the beginning of the entry.

Biographies are prepared by Omnigraphics editors after extensive research, utilizing the most current materials available. Those sources that are generally available to students appear in the list of further reading at the end of the sketch.

Indexes

To provide easy access to entries, each issue of the regular *Biography Today* series and each volume of the Special Subject Series contains a Name Index, General Index covering occupations, organizations, and ethnic and minority origins, Places of Birth Index, and a Birthday Index. These indexes cumulate with each succeeding volume or issue. Each of the Special Subject Volumes will be indexed as part of these cumulative indexes, so that readers can locate information on all individuals covered in either the regular or the special volumes. A "Guide to the Indexes" appears on page 161.

Our Advisors

This member of the *Biography Today* family of publications was reviewed by an Advisory Board comprised of librarians, children's literature specialists, and reading instructors so that we could make sure that the concept of this publication — to provide a readable and accessible biographical magazine for young readers — was on target. They evaluated the title as it developed, and their suggestions have proved invaluable. Any errors, however, are ours alone. We'd like to list the Advisory Board members, and to thank them for their efforts.

Sandra Arden, *Retired*
Assistant Director
Troy Public Library, Troy, MI

Gail Beaver
Ann Arbor Huron High School Library
and the University of Michigan School
of Information and Library Studies
Ann Arbor, MI

Marilyn Bethel
Pompano Beach Branch Library
Pompano Beach, FL

Eileen Butterfield
Waterford Public Library
Waterford, CT

Linda Carpino
Detroit Public Library
Detroit, MI

Helen Gregory
Grosse Pointe Public Library
Grosse Pointe, MI

Jane Klasing, *Retired*
School Board of Broward County,
Fort Lauderdale, FL

Marlene Lee
Broward County Public Library System,
Fort Lauderdale, FL

Judy Liskov
Waterford Public Library
Waterford, CT

Sylvia Mavrogenes
Miami-Dade Public Library System
Miami, FL

Carole J. McCollough
Wayne State University School of
Library Science, Detroit, MI

Deborah Rutter
Russell Library, Middletown, CT

Barbara Sawyer
Groton Public Library and Information
Center, Groton, CT

Renee Schwartz
School Board of Broward County
Fort Lauderdale, FL

Lee Sprince
Broward West Regional Library
Fort Lauderdale, FL

Susan Stewart, *Retired*
Birney Middle School Reading
Laboratory, Southfield, MI

Ethel Stoloff, *Retired*
Librarian, Birney Middle School,
Southfield, MI

Our Advisory Board stressed to us that we should not shy away from controversial or unconventional people in our profiles, and we have tried to follow their advice. The Advisory Board also mentioned that the sketches might be useful in reluctant reader and adult literacy programs, and we would value any comments librarians might have about the suitability of our magazine for those purposes.

Your Comments Are Welcome

Our goal is to be accurate and up-to-date, to give young readers information they can learn from and enjoy. Now we want to know what you think. Take a look at this issue of *Biography Today,* on approval. Write or call me with your comments. We want to provide an excellent source of biographical information for young people. Let us know how you think we're doing.

And here's a special incentive: review our list of people to appear in upcoming issues. Use the bind-in card to list other people you want to see in *Biography Today*. If we include someone you suggest, your library wins a free issue, with our thanks. Please see the bind-in card for details.

Laurie Harris
Executive Editor, *Biography Today*

Jane Brody 1941-

American Journalist and Science Writer
Author of Books and Columns for the *New York Times*
on Issues Relating to Diet, Nutrition, and Personal
Health

BIRTH

Jane Ellen Brody was born in Brooklyn, New York, on May 19,
1941. Her parents were Sidney Brody, a lawyer and civil servant,
and Lillian (Kellner) Brody, an elementary school teacher. Brody
had one younger brother, Jeffrey.

YOUTH

Growing up in Brooklyn, Brody showed an interest in science while still very young. She got a lot of support for that interest from her father, as she recalls here. "When at age four I told my father I wanted to be a veterinarian, he didn't say girls don't become veterinarians (which was true in 1945). He said, 'Cornell [University in western New York] has a College of Veterinary Medicine.' And I grew up thinking I would go to Cornell and become a vet."

That was an unusual attitude for the era. Brody grew up at a time when most American women didn't work outside the home. The men went off to work each day, while the women stayed home to take care of their children and their house. Brody's childhood wasn't like that; she says that she grew up in "a truly liberated household." Her mother always worked outside the home, and her father helped with the shopping, cooking, and washing up. Brody always assumed that she would work, too. "I never had the feeling that things were not appropriate for me to do," she recalls. "There were never those kinds of barriers, either emotionally or intellectually." That egalitarian atmosphere, she says, helped her develop her levelheaded attitude and independent spirit.

> ——— " ———
>
> *When she was younger, Brody recalls, "I never sat down at my desk before I had put some money into the candy machine. Eating at that point had nothing whatever to do with physical hunger; it had to do with emotional hunger. I was unhappy, and food was the only thing that made me feel good."*
>
> ——— " ———

Her father encouraged that egalitarian attitude and supported her in other ways as well, as Brody recalls here. "It was my father who taught me to swim at age three and roller-skate at four, who took me bicycling riding and hiking, who bought me an Erector set and a chemistry set and who supported my interest in nature and baseball." Through his support, she grew to believe that girls, like boys, need all types of activities, including those that challenge their intellect and those that channel their physical energy.

Brody, who is now well known for her writings on proper diet and nutrition, learned both unhealthy and healthy food habits as a child. The family ate many heavy traditional Jewish and Eastern European foods, with an emphasis on such fat-laden and artery-clogging items as butter and chicken fat. Brody once admitted that she ate whole sticks of butter and blocks of Velveeta cheese as a child. But there were some positive lessons, too. "My father always had a passion for certain healthy things. Fresh fruit in every season, and dark bread. We ate oatmeal in winter and shredded wheat in summer."

In Brody's family, food had an important emotional component as well. "My grandmother was always trying to fatten me up. In my home food was synonymous with love, and people always tried to get me to eat more than I wanted." As a child, Brody began a struggle with her weight that continued throughout much of her early life.

EDUCATION

Brody attended New York State College of Agriculture at Cornell University, where she majored in biochemistry. At first, she intended to become a research scientist. Then she spent a summer working as a National Science Foundation fellow at the New York State Agricultural Experiment Station in Geneva, New York. After a summer alone running a research experiment, she became convinced that "what was fun for 10 weeks, when projected to 10 years, was not so enticing. I could see myself shortly talking to test tubes." Brody realized that "science happens *very* slowly — and is very lonely. I really liked people better than test tubes."

Another experience helped her change her mind about a career as a research scientist. At Cornell, Brody recalls, she felt lost and unconnected to the rest of the college community. She spoke to a psychologist, who suggested that she join the staff of the *Cornell Countryman*, a school magazine. She began writing about science and agricultural research, and even volunteered to be editor of the magazine. She had what she has called an "aha!" experience: "One day I said, 'This is what I really love, finding out what other researchers are doing.'" Writing about science, she found, provided both stimulating scientific content and personal contact with other scientists. And she soon discovered that she had a knack for conveying complex scientific information in a clear, easy-to-understand manner. In 1962 Brody earned her bachelor of science degree from Cornell University. She graduated with distinction, the second highest in her class.

Brody then enrolled in a one-year master's program at the University of Wisconsin's School of Journalism under a science writing fellowship. At Wisconsin, she was assigned to news about the university's medical school. During that year, she assembled a large file of newspaper clippings of her writings about medicine. She earned her master's degree in science journalism from the University of Wisconsin in 1963.

FIRST JOBS

Brody's hard work in journalism school paid off. Her extensive clippings file, plus her unique combination of writing skills and science background, helped

her land a job at the *Minneapolis Tribune*. She worked there from 1963 to 1965 as a general assignment reporter, specializing in science. But she became frustrated by the lack of important scientific or medical stories occurring there. After spending most of her time on general assignments, Brody knew that she would have to move to a larger city to be able to cover the kind of stories that interested her.

Her time in Minneapolis proved difficult on a more personal level as well. "I wasn't used to Midwestern reticence," says Brody. "I felt very isolated and different. So I turned to food." Her problems with her weight were becoming more acute.

STRUGGLING WITH HER WEIGHT

Brody had been struggling with her weight throughout her years of growing up, going to college, and starting to work. Since Brody is exactly five feet tall and just over 100 pounds today, it's hard to imagine that she once had trouble with her weight. The problem started early. She was heavy throughout her childhood and teen years. During her freshman year in college, she started out eating everything in sight. Determined to get her weight under control, she went on a sensible diet during the summer after that first year and managed to take the weight off. She kept it off successfully for several years, until she finished college and started graduate school in Wisconsin. She started gaining weight while in school in Wisconsin and continued when she was working in Minneapolis, until she was about 35 to 40 pounds overweight. "I never sat down at my desk before I had put some money into the candy machine. Eating at that point had nothing whatever to do with physical hunger; it had to do with emotional hunger. I was unhappy, and food was the only thing that made me feel good."

Brody was a compulsive eater. Often she would try not to eat all day, but then she would eat all night. She ate when she was depressed, anxious, bored, or frustrated. She tried all types of diets, all without success. "When I ran out of diets, I concocted my own," Brody says. "During one period I ate only liver, grapefruit, and graham crackers. In fact, I ate so many graham crackers that I developed an allergy to them. After that, I went through a period when I wouldn't eat anything all day until supper and then I couldn't stop eating until I went to bed. I ate past the point of pain in my stomach because the food felt so good in my mouth."

Finally, after about three years of this, she started to become seriously worried about her health. "I was killing myself slowly, and I knew I had to do something to stop," Brody says. One night in late 1965 she reached a breaking point. "I remember waking up in the middle of the night afraid that I wouldn't live to see the next morning. I called a therapist right then and there and asked for help. He said he'd see me first thing in the morning, and that got me through the night."

By November 1965, Brody was ready to make a profound change in her life. She quit dieting and started eating sensibly. "I decided that if I was going to be fat, at least I was going to be healthy. From that day on, I started eating regular meals and always carried a healthy snack with me." She started eating three healthy meals each day, with lots of fresh fruits and vegetables. She also started exercising regularly, including tennis, jogging, ice skating, swimming, and bicycling. Much to her surprise, she began losing weight. She lost 10 pounds the first month, and the rest of the 40 pounds over the next two years. She has never gained the weight back.

CAREER HIGHLIGHTS

The year 1965 was a time of big changes for Brody. In addition to starting a new health regimen and weight loss program, she also started a new job. While working at the *Minneapolis Tribune,* she went back to New York on vacation to see her family. There was an opening for a science writer at the *New York Times,* one of the nation's top newspapers. Her family encouraged her to go in for an interview, but Brody expected it to be pointless. With only two years of work experience in Minnesota, she was still a fairly inexperienced reporter, not yet considered qualified for a job at the *Times.* At the interview, she was asked if she would write women's news; she said no. The editor, A.M. Rosenthal, told her that she had "a lot of nerve" to be applying for the science writer job, since the other applicants had 20 years of experience. Brody recalls that interview here. "I said, 'Mr. Rosenthal, if I didn't think I could do this job I wouldn't be here' — and as I said it I thought what am I saying? — but that was exactly what he wanted to hear. He liked my writing, and he also liked what can only be called chutzpah." Brody was only 24 when she started at the *New York Times.*

She started out at the *Times* in 1965 as a science writer. In that position, she wrote articles on a wide range of scientific subjects. While Brody enjoyed her work, she had strong feelings about the types of science writing that she should be doing. "My feeling from the day I was hired was that the *Times* needed to do more popular medicine: to help people to understand how their bodies work. I felt that people needed to know not just how to recognize disease but how to stay well." That idea came to fruition in 1976, when she was asked by the *Times* to begin writing a weekly column, "Personal Health." The column is now syndicated, appearing in 100 newspapers around the country.

Writing on Health Issues

Brody's "Personal Health" columns frequently express her philosophy about good health. First and foremost, she believes that each individual is responsible for maintaining their own health — by educating themselves about major issues and by making choices that ensure good health. Much of the health care system is designed not to care for health, in fact, but instead to care for disease. And many of the most important illnesses today are directly related to lifestyle issues, which people can control. As Brody explains it, "We are living in a society that is spending over $300 billion a year on medical care, only we're not getting health care for that $300 billion. We're getting sickness care.

Health care is a whole other story. We give people immunizations and say we're preventing disease, which indeed we're doing. But it's not those diseases that are killing Americans. It's heart disease and cancer and stroke and high blood pressure and diabetes and other chronic illnesses. These diseases we can do something about because our risk in developing them is influenced by *how we live our lives*."

———— **"** ————

Throughout her columns, Brody has thoroughly explored this relationship of how we need to live our lives in order to maintain our health. She has developed a philosophy of healthy living, which is based both on her own experiences and on current scientific thinking. She believes there are several key elements of a healthy lifestyle. Diet and nutrition is one key element. Brody recommends a daily diet that is high in fresh fruits, vegetables, and complex carbohydrates—things like rice, beans, pasta, cereal, potatoes, bread, and whole grains. She recommends eating very little sugar and fat and taking smaller portions of protein, particularly limiting meat, which is high in fat. She believes in eating regular, healthful meals rather than depriving oneself of good food. But she also emphasizes moderation, saying that an occasional small helping of cookies or ice cream won't destroy you. In addition Brody also emphasizes the importance of minimizing stress in your life and exercising regularly. This last item is particularly important, because exercise helps to strength and condition the body, to control weight, and to relieve stress.

"We are living in a society that is spending over $300 billion a year on medical care, only we're not getting health care for that $300 billion. We're getting sickness care. Health care is a whole other story. We give people immunizations and say we're preventing disease, which indeed we're doing. But it's not those diseases that are killing Americans. It's heart disease and cancer and stroke and high blood pressure and diabetes and other chronic illnesses. These diseases we can do something about because our risk in developing them is influenced by **how we live our lives."**

———— **"** ————

How Brody Goes about Her Work

Brody works out of her home in Brooklyn, New York. She does all her own research, scanning approximately 30 scientific journals and other publications each week to keep up with current research. She often calls the scientists directly to ask for further information on their projects. She gets her ideas for columns in different ways: from her friends, acquaintances, and colleagues, from her reading, from news events, and from her readers' letters. "I work on the principle of critical mass," she explains. "When I get an idea I start gathering data. It may be three years later that I can take all the material home and make a few phone calls and synthesize the information."

Brody has developed a reputation for adept selection of topics, fair and balanced reporting of controversial issues, and thorough research and accuracy. Her ability to synthesize ideas from different sources and different disciplines, along with her ability to present that complex information in a style that is clear and easy to understand, has won her the respect of doctors, scientists, and many loyal readers. According to Robert Barnett, an editor of *American Health*, "She has done more than any other journalist to bring accurate information about nutrition and health to the public." She receives many letters — from doctors and patients — thanking her for explaining medical issues. Often, her columns inspire readers to get medical help that they may not have known they needed. Brody recalls one such instance here. "One 17-year-old girl read my article on a blinding eye disorder and convinced her mother she should see an ophthalmologist. She was found to have a detached retina, which was welded back, and her sight was saved."

> ❝
>
> *"I want to be remembered as a person who cared deeply about the well-being of my fellow inhabitants on this Earth. And who had done the best I could to help people die young — as late in life as possible."*
>
> ❞

Brody's fans particularly enjoy her column's many references to her own experiences. Recently, for example, she confessed that she had realized that she wasn't getting enough sleep. She was so tired, in fact, that she had even fallen asleep in the middle of a phone interview she was conducting with a scientist! Typically for Brody, she used her experience as an opportunity to do research on sleep requirements. She determined that she was sleep deprived, changed her personal habits to include getting more sleep, and then wrote about it in her column.

In addition to her articles for the *New York Times*, Brody has also been involved in several other projects that have expanded her audience. She has written health columns for magazines and is also a popular speaker on the lecture circuit. In 1981 she published *Jane Brody's Nutrition Book*, which explained and summarized her views on good nutrition. It spent 20 weeks on the bestseller list. She followed that up in 1985 with *Jane Brody's Good Food Book: Living the High-Carbohydrate Way*, which is really two books in one. The first part is a summary of nutrition principles and an extensive description of starchy foods, including some that are little known. That is followed by a section on how to equip a kitchen, how to fill a pantry, and how to shop. The second part is a cookbook containing recipes that embody her nutrition principles. Both food experts and the general public were impressed with her ability to combine healthy eating with great taste. Brody has gone on to write cookbooks devoted to entertaining and to seafood, as well as health guides devoted to colds and flu, allergies, and general health issues.

Now in her mid-50s, Brody isn't ready to retire yet. But she has thought ahead to that point, imagining what her legacy will be. "I want to be remembered as a person who cared deeply about the well-being of my fellow inhabitants on this Earth," Brody says. "And who had done the best I could to help people die young—as late in life as possible."

MARRIAGE AND FAMILY

Brody married Richard Engquist, a song lyricist and playwright, on October 2, 1966. They have twin sons, Lee Erik and Lorin Michael. When the boys were young, Richard started working at home so he could take care of them. "Richard is a very crucial element in making my life possible," Brody says, "because we really do share household tasks." Early on, she incorporated her views on good nutrition into her family's diet, and Erik and Lorin were often her first taste testers when she was trying new recipes. Like their mom, they have learned to prefer the whole-grain, low-fat approach to food.

HOBBIES AND OTHER INTERESTS

Because she works at home, Brody has the flexibility to enjoy the benefits of exercise at convenient times during the day. She starts her day early, but then takes breaks from her work to enjoy tennis, biking, running, swimming, and ice skating.

WRITINGS

Secrets of Good Health, 1970 (with Richard Engquist)
You Can Fight Cancer and Win, 1977 (with Arthur I. Holleb)
Jane Brody's Nutrition Book, 1981
Jane Brody's 'The New York Times' Guide to Personal Health, 1982
Jane Brody's Good Food Book: Living the High Carbohydrate Way, 1985
Jane Brody's Good Food Gourmet, 1990
Jane Brody's Good Seafood Book, 1994 (with Richard Flaste)
Jane Brody's Cold and Flu Fighter, 1995

Jane Brody's Allergy Fighter, 1997
'The New York Times' Book of Health: How to Feel Fitter, Eat Better, and Live Longer, 1997

HONORS AND AWARDS

Howard Blakeslee Award (American Heart Association): 1971
Science Writers' Award (American Dental Association): 1971, 1978
J.C. Penney-University of Missouri Journalism Award: 1978
Lifeline Award (American Health Foundation): 1978

FURTHER READING

Books

Braden, Maria. *She Said What? Interviews with Women Newspaper Columnists,* 1993
Contemporary Authors New Revision Series, Vol. 23
Grolier Library of North American Biographies: Scientists, Vol. 8, 1994
Who's Who in America, 1997
Writers Directory, 1994-96

Periodicals

Current Biography Yearbook 1986
50 Plus, Mar. 1984, p.28
Harper's, May 1982, p.12
New York Times, Sep. 22, 1981, p. ; May 29, 1991, p.C10
Newsweek, Aug. 4, 1986, p.58
Publisher's Weekly, Oct. 18, 1985, p.65
Time, Nov. 10, 1986, p.98
Weight Watchers Magazine, Nov. 1984, p.24

ADDRESS

The New York Times
229 West 43rd Street
New York, NY 10036

OBITUARY

Seymour Cray 1925-1996

American Computer Designer
Creator of the First "Supercomputer"

BIRTH

Seymour Roger Cray was born on September 28, 1925, in Chippewa Falls, a small town in the heart of Wisconsin's dairy country. His father was a city engineer in Chippewa Falls, and his mother was a homemaker. Seymour's sister, Carol, was born five years later.

YOUTH

Although Seymour had a typical midwestern boyhood, he was anything but a typical midwestern boy. By the age of 10, he had built an automatic telegraph machine that could translate punched paper tape into Morse Code, which he used to communicate with his sister in another bedroom. His parents did everything they could to support his interest in science, setting up a laboratory for him in the basement furnished with chemistry sets and radio equipment. Seymour wasted no time wiring his lab to his bedroom, so that an electric alarm would go off every time someone tried to enter his room.

EDUCATION

Seymour Cray attended Chippewa Falls High School. He sang in the Boys' Glee Club, but he avoided sports and wasn't interested in girls. His passion was science, and he was often asked to teach the physics class in his teacher's absence. When he graduated in 1943, he received the Bausch & Lomb Science Award.

Cray finished high school in the middle of World War II, so after graduation he served in the U.S. Army. He put his talent for electronics to good use as a radio operator in Europe and as a code-breaker in the Philippines for Japanese radio transmissions. After World War II, he enrolled at the University of Wisconsin in Madison. But he soon transferred to the University of Minnesota, where he received a bachelor's degree in electrical engineering in 1950 and a master's degree in applied mathematics the following year.

> *Cray admits that as a college student, he was "one of those nerds before the word became popular. I spent all my time in the electrical engineering laboratory, and not enough time socializing."*

Cray admits that as a college student, he was "one of those nerds before the word became popular. I spent all my time in the electrical engineering laboratory, and not enough time socializing." His main concern was that because he used a circular slide rule rather than the straight kind his classmates carried in a leather case hanging from their belts, people wouldn't recognize him as a future engineer.

FIRST JOBS

After graduating from college, Cray went to work for Engineering Research Associates (ERA) in St. Paul, Minnesota. Working out of a converted wooden glider factory, the company was involved in designing the first commercial computers. With his extensive knowledge of circuits, logic, and computer software design, Cray helped design the UNIVAC 1103, the first digital computer to be sold commercially. He also designed one of the first scientific computers, the ERA 1101, used to solve complex scientific equations.

Within two years of hiring Cray, ERA merged with another company that was more interested in making smaller, less expensive computers. So Cray and William Norris, ERA's founder and Cray's first mentor, left in 1957 to set up their own company, Control Data Corporation (CDC).

CAREER HIGHLIGHTS

Seymour Cray's career spanned the entire history of computers. A pioneer in his field, he was always on the leading edge, creating the fastest and most powerful technology. Computer technology has changed in a revolutionary way since Cray started out in the 1950s. Personal Computers (PCs) didn't even exist at that time. The only computers that did exist were large bulky machines that filled a whole room (although they didn't have nearly as much power as a typical PC today). These large computers used vacuum tubes to electrically store and process information. But that technology changed over the years. Eventually, vacuum tubes were replaced by transistors, which were cheaper, more reliable, used less power, and were much smaller. These gave way to semiconductors, which could hold 50,000 or more transistors on a single chip. Today, large computer chips have millions of transistors.

At Control Data

Because Control Data was just getting started, Cray set out to make computers as cheaply as he could. Instead of the hot, bulky vacuum tubes that made most early computers fill an entire room, he used transistors, which he purchased at a local electronics store for 37 cents each. The transistors were not only more reliable, but they also made it possible to build a much smaller computer. The CDC 1604, which came out in 1958, was the first commercial computer to use individual transistors instead of vacuum tubes. It could perform high-speed, extremely accurate arithmetic, yet it cost considerably less than other computers that weren't as fast. In less than two years, CDC was showing a profit.

Although Seymour Cray's reputation as a computer designer was growing, he had no patience for the administrative tasks involved in business. So in 1962, William Norris built him a laboratory on a 40-acre piece of land near his home in Chippewa Falls. Cray became a hermit, designing his computers with only a pencil and a pad of graph paper. He would fill an entire pad each day with his calculations, to be built by his development team. Because he didn't want his work to be interrupted, Cray allowed Norris to visit him only twice a year.

Seymour Cray with the S/N 1 Cray-1 Computer System, 1976

By August 1963, when the CDC 6600 was announced, Cray had designed the most powerful computer of its time. It was capable of carrying out three million "floating-point operations" (flops) per second, or three Megaflops. (A "floating point operation" is the addition, subtraction, multiplication, or division of two numbers of the type used in scientific notation, such as 1.345 x 10^{11}.) It was also the first computer to use Freon—the same liquid coolant used in refrigerators and air conditioners—to keep its 350,000 transistors from overheating. Within five years, 63 of these state-of-the-art machines were being used by organizations involved in scientific research.

Cray went on to design the CDC 7600, which was even more powerful, and then the 8600, which the company chose not to market because it wanted to focus on smaller, more commercial computers. Once again, Seymour Cray decided it was time to strike out on his own. He left CDC in 1972 to set up his own company, Cray Research Corporation.

The First Supercomputer

Cray insisted that his new company build only supercomputers and that they be built one at a time. "Supercomputer" is a term generally used to describe the fastest, most powerful computer — and usually the most expensive — in existence. More specifically, supercomputers at that time were those that could perform more than 20 Megaflops.

Because they can perform complex mathematical calculations so quickly, supercomputers are able to do simulations. This type of computer modeling combines theory with experimentation — all on the computer. They can simulate physical events in three dimensions — such as the path of a speeding bullet or a developing tornado. But they cost so much (usually millions of dollars) that only government laboratories, universities, and large corporations can afford to buy them. They are invaluable, however, when it comes to such complex tasks as designing new drugs and safer cars, forecasting the weather, exploring underground oil reserves, and testing nuclear weapons. They allow engineers to play elaborate "what if" games on their computer screens, thus saving the time, money, and potential danger involved in trying out each option for real.

The Cray-1

The first supercomputer Seymour Cray designed for his new company, the Cray-1, was released in 1976. It was about 10 times faster than any computer then in existence. The Cray-1 was capable of working on many different parts of a problem at once, at a speed of about 130 Megaflops. It was six feet high and eight feet in diameter, and it had more than 200,000 semiconductor chips and 60 miles of wiring inside. Shaped like a cylinder with a padded bench around the outside, it was often referred to as "the world's most expensive loveseat." Six of the machines were sold during the late 1970s, including one to the federal research center at Los Alamos, New Mexico, where it was used to simulate nuclear explosions.

Cray Research was very successful with their new supercomputers. They sold 23 of them in 1984 alone, putting the company at the top of the supercomputer industry. But as the company grew, Cray again felt that he was spending too much time managing people and not enough time designing new computers. He turned over the day-to-day responsibility for running the company to others and went to work as an independent contractor. Once again, he returned to Chippewa Falls, where he could work without interruption on designing the successor to the Cray-1.

Cray-2

The Cray-2, completed in 1985, was about 10 times faster than the Cray-1 and about 40,000-50,000 times faster than the personal computers of its day. It had the largest internal memory capacity of any computer in existence, and it performed at a speed of 1,000 Megaflops (one Gigaflop). Problems that had taken scientists a year or more to solve in the early 1950s could now be solved in a second. The Cray-2 was used to design heat shields for spacecraft and to study the intense magnetic fields required for fusion reactors. What's more, it fit into a C-shaped cabinet only 53 inches across and 45 inches high. And that smaller size was important.

For a computer to be fast, it had to be small. The speed of computer chips had reached a point where the time it took for electrical impulses to travel the length of the computer limited the computer's speed as a whole. By packing 240,000 computer chips into such a small space, Cray was able to minimize the distance electrical impulses had to travel and thus make his machine much faster. According to the *New York Times*, Cray was "a genius in the art of dense packaging of the components that make up a computer, a design approach that slashes the time it takes electrical signals to travel between circuits." To overcome the problem of the heat generated by the tightly packed circuit boards, he flooded the computer with a liquid coolant, which could be seen gurgling behind its glass walls. One owner of the Cray-2 nicknamed its computer "Bubbles."

The Cray-3 and After

By 1990, four out of every five supercomputers in the world were designed by Seymour Cray. But the market was changing. Competition from the Japanese was increasing, and many U.S. companies were making smaller, less expensive machines that were able to perform many of the same tasks as supercomputers. Also, the market for PCs for home use was changing the focus of the industry. The large corporations and government agencies who were once Cray's best customers were turning their attention to "parallel processing"—linking together smaller computers with powerful microprocessors to match the speed of supercomputers—while Cray insisted on sticking with "vector processing"—creating one large, fast machine capable of working on many different parts of the problem at once. And the end of the Cold War meant that supercomputers were no longer as essential to the defense industry.

The chairman of Cray Research, John Rollwagen, began to worry about the company's future. He had been pouring money into the Cray-3 project, which was already behind schedule and over budget. He finally chose Steve S. Chen,

The Cray-2 Computer System, 1984

a talented young computer designer, to develop the company's next super-computer, the C-90. Rollwagen told Cray that he'd give him $150 million in cash and equipment to set up a new company that would continue work on the Cray-3. So in 1989, Cray moved to Colorado Springs and established Cray Computer. His goal was to complete work on the Cray-3 and its successor, the Cray-4.

Seymour Cray's need to outdo himself every time he designed a new comput-er led him to pursue increasingly risky projects. Unlike Chen's C-90 (and the current generation of PCs), which were based on silicon computer chips, the Cray-3 used chips made from gallium arsenide, which produced less heat and operated at higher speeds but were much more difficult to work with. Problems with the Cray-3's electrical connections and cooling system caused further delays. In December 1991, Cray Computer missed a crucial deadline and lost its only customer for the new machine. The company was eventually forced to file for bankruptcy in March 1995.

Never losing faith in his own ability to start over, Seymour Cray established his fourth company, SRC Computer (his own initials), in the summer of 1996. But on September 22, he was severely injured in a car accident in Colorado Springs. Cray died two weeks later, on October 5, 1996. He was 71.

A Legendary Figure

At the time of his unexpected death, Cray was already a legendary figure in the computer world. Although he once described himself as "a plumber," he has often been compared to Thomas Edison and other famous American inventors. No other computer scientist has been able to design an entire supercomputer in his head, as Cray routinely did, and few have been as dedicated to their work. Cray refused to give speeches to business or scientific groups, and he granted very few interviews. He disconnected his phone every afternoon so he wouldn't be distracted, and he avoided publicity whenever possible. He even refused to show up at the White House to receive a national science award.

When it came to conducting business, Cray believed in simplicity and directness. A vice president at Control Data once asked him to produce a one-year and a five-year development plan. The next day, Cray handed him two three-ring binders, each containing a single sheet of paper. In the binder labeled "Five-Year Plan" he had written, "To build the world's fastest computers." The sheet of paper in the second binder read, "To complete one-fifth of the five-year plan."

Because he worked in seclusion for most of his life, many stories were passed around about Cray. In fact, he has become somewhat of a legend, and it's unclear which, if any, of the stories are true. One story was that he built an elaborate network of tunnels beneath his house in Chippewa Falls, and that when he got stumped on a design problem at work, he would go home and dig for a while. Another was that when Cray wanted to buy a new car, he would walk into the showroom and choose the first model to his right. Perhaps the most famous of the legends surrounding Cray was that he would design and build a new wooden sailboat every winter in his basement, launch it in the spring, and then set fire to it on the beach at the end of the summer

> ———— " ————
>
> *According to Elizabeth Corcoran, "Building computers was his livelihood — but it was also his passion. Cray designed the machines to suit his whimsy, each time challenging his imagination to do something that hadn't been done before — to build the fastest machine in the world. Throughout the years, he designed with the joyfulness of a young man in love — ablaze with new ideas, unencumbered by earlier mistakes. For that, many in the engineering and scientific worlds thought of him as a hero."*
>
> ———— " ————

so it wouldn't influence his design for a new boat. Whether or not it is true, this story says a great deal about his approach to designing computers.

Cray's Legacy

Cray will be remembered as one of the pioneers of the computer industry. He was renowned for building the fastest computers in existence and for creating innovative technologies that were later used by the rest of the industry. But he was also acclaimed for the simplicity and elegance of his designs.

Here, Elizabeth Corcoran offers an appreciation for Cray's achievements in the *Washington Post*: "According to the old saying, if a man made a better mousetrap, the world would beat a path to his door. Even if he lived in the woods.

"For decades, Seymour Cray lived up to that adage. From a lab in rural Chip pewa Falls, Wis., he designed the Lamborghinis of the computer world and gave them his surname. Building computers was his livelihood—but it was also his passion. Cray designed the machines to suit his whimsy, each time challenging his imagination to do something that hadn't been done before— to build the fastest machine in the world.

"Throughout the years," Corcoran writes, "he designed with the joyfulness of a young man in love—ablaze with new ideas, unencumbered by earlier mistakes. For that, many in the engineering and scientific worlds thought of him as a hero."

MARRIAGE AND FAMILY

Cray was married twice. His first wife, Verene, was a minister's daughter whom he married shortly after his discharge from the Army. They had two daughters, Susan and Carolyn, and a son, Steven. Verene worked hard to maintain a sense of family togetherness despite Cray's obsessive work schedule. Although she expected him to be at the table for dinner each night, he was usually back in his lab as soon after as he could manage, working well past midnight. The children remember having to maintain total silence on long car trips so he could concentrate on solving computer design problems. They were even scolded for fiddling with the car ashtrays. His eldest daughter, Susan, recalls leaving questions about her algebra homework on her father's desk in the evening, knowing that she'd find the answers waiting for her in the morning. In 1975, the Crays were divorced.

The following year, Cray met Geri Harrand, the owner of a physical therapy business. They were married in 1980. Geri urged him to get out of his lab more often and encouraged him to develop new interests. And Cray listened. He took up skiing, windsurfing, and sailing, and they also traveled widely.

HOBBIES AND OTHER INTERESTS

Although he had limited time for activities that didn't involve designing computers, Cray enjoyed sailing and windsurfing. For a while, he was fascinated by boomerangs and tried to build the world's largest — six feet across.

Cray was a devoted fan of "Star Trek," the 1960s television series about space travel. When he finished building the first Cray-2 in 1985, a number of people remarked that its futuristic-looking cabinet closely resembled the transporter machine on his favorite TV show.

HONORS AND AWARDS

Harry Goode Memorial Award: 1972, for outstanding achievement in the
field of information processing
National Inventors Hall of Fame: 1997

FURTHER READING

Books
Encyclopedia Britannica, 1995
Murray, Charles J. *The Supermen: The Story of Seymour Cray and the Technical
Wizards behind the Superconductor,* 1997
Notable Twentieth-Century Scientists, 1995
Slater, Robert. *Portraits in Silicon,* 1987
Who's Who in America, 1996

Periodicals
Business Week, Apr. 30, 1990, p.80
Computerworld, June 22, 1992, p.38; July 18, 1994, p.20; Oct. 24, 1996, p.4;
Nov. 4, 1996, p.157
Electronic News, Oct. 14, 1996, p.1
Los Angeles Times, June 4, 1989, Business Section, p.1; Sep. 24, 1996, p.D1
New York Times, May 21, 1989, Business Section, p.1; Oct. 6, 1996, p.47
Philadelphia Inquirer, Oct. 6, 1996, p.E4
Time, June 17, 1985, p.53; Mar. 28, 1988, p.54; May 29, 1989, p.70
USA Today, Sep. 25, 1996, p.4B
Washington Post, Oct. 6, 1996, p.B6; Oct. 7, 1996, p.C1

WORLD WIDE WEB SITE
http://www.cray.com

OBITUARY

Paul Erdös 1913-1996

Hungarian-Born Mathematician
Pioneer in the Fields of Number Theory and
Combinatorics

BIRTH

Paul Erdös (AIR-dish) was born on March 26, 1913, in Budapest,
Hungary. His parents, Lajos Erdös and Anna (Wilhelm) Erdös,
were both high school math teachers. While Anna Erdös was in
the hospital giving birth to Paul, her two other children, Clara
and Magda, died of scarlet fever at the ages of three and five. The

loss of her daughters was something Anna Erdös never liked to talk about. All Paul knew about his sisters was that they were considered to be "the smart ones."

YOUTH

Not long after the outbreak of World War I, Lajos Erdös was taken prisoner by the Russians and sent to Siberia for several years. Young Paul, who was not yet two years old at the time, was raised by his mother until he was almost eight. Anna Erdös doted on her only remaining child, and she and the family's servants did everything for him. He was 11 years old before he learned to tie his own shoes and 21 before he had to butter his own bread. Even as an adult, he had no idea how to take care of himself.

Paul grew up totally immersed in the world of mathematics. By the time he was three, he could multiply three- and four-digit numbers in his head. He would often amuse himself by solving math problems that he'd made up, such as how long it would take for a train to travel to the sun. He entertained his parents' friends by asking them how old they were and then, without a moment's hesitation, telling them how many seconds they had lived. Because both of his parents were math teachers, young Paul had an opportunity to meet many of the great Hungarian mathematicians of the day.

EARLY MEMORIES

Erdös clearly remembered having his first mathematical insight at the age of four. Although he didn't yet know how to write numbers, he could perform calculations in his head. He turned to his mother one day and said, "If you subtract 250 from 100, you get 150 below zero." No one had ever explained the concept of negative numbers to Paul, yet he was able to grasp it on his own.

EDUCATION

Erdös had an unconventional education. His mother took him out of grammar school because she was convinced that it was full of germs and that he would fall prey to various childhood diseases if he stayed there. Even in high school, his mother kept changing her mind about whether it was a safe place for him to be. He ended up spending most of his high school years at home, where his parents tutored him.

Despite his lack of formal schooling, Erdös entered the University of Budapest at the age of 17 and graduated four years later with a Ph.D. in math. The work he did there caught the attention of Louis Mordell, a mathematician at

Manchester University in England. Erdös accepted Mordell's offer of a post-doctoral fellowship at Manchester, and he spent the next four years in England. "I left Hungary for political reasons," he once said. "I was Jewish, and Hungary was a semi-fascist country. But I was very homesick, so I went back three times a year."

As Hungary and surrounding nations fell under the influence of Nazi Germany in the 1930s, Europe became an increasingly dangerous place for all Jews, including Erdös. In 1938, his fellowship at Manchester University ended. That same year, Adolf Hitler, the Nazi dictator of Germany, took control of parts of Czechoslovakia and invaded Austria. Rather than returning home at the end of his stay in England, therefore, Erdös decided to go to America and spend a year at the Institute for Advanced Study at Princeton University. During World War II, the Nazis ended up murdering four of his mother's five brothers and sisters, and his father died of a heart attack in 1942. His mother survived the war, although he wasn't able to see her again until 1948. For the next several decades, he was unable to return home for more than a brief visit.

CAREER HIGHLIGHTS

Erdös's fellowship at Princeton lasted from 1938 until 1939. When it ended he accepted short-term appointments at Notre Dame, Purdue, Stanford, the University of Pennsylvania, and other universities, which kept him in the United States throughout the 1940s. But when he wanted to attend a conference in 1954 in Amsterdam, the U.S. government would not allow him to return because of international politics, the fear of communism, and the situation in his birthplace, Hungary.

"Mathematicians on four continents have made Erdös's well-being their collective responsibility," John Tierney wrote. "They see it as their duty to mathematics."

After World War II, the Soviet Union and the U.S. engaged in what was known as the "Cold War." The Soviets had taken over most of Eastern Europe following the war, setting up communist governments in each country, including Hungary. Anti-communist feeling was very strong in the U.S. at the time, and Hungary was considered a communist country. Here, Erdös describes what happened when he tried to get a re-entry permit to return to the U.S. after the conference in Amsterdam. "The immigrations officials asked me all sorts of silly questions. 'Have you read [Karl] Marx, [Friedrich] Engels, or [Joseph] Stalin?' 'No,' I said. 'What do you think of Marx?' they pressed. 'I'm not competent to judge,' I said, 'but no doubt he was a great man.' So they denied me a re-entry visa. I had the classic American reaction: I left." Erdös went to Israel, where he stayed for much of the 1950s. He was finally allowed to return to the U.S. in 1963.

Life as a Wandering Mathematician

From the 1960s on, Paul Erdös lived primarily in the United States, visiting Budapest in the summers and spending long periods in Israel, Canada, and England. But from that time on, he never had an official job anywhere. Throughout his life, he never had a house or apartment of his own. Instead, he lived as a wandering mathematician. His mother traveled everywhere with him beginning in 1964, when she was 84; they continued this way until her death in 1971.

Erdös would visit his colleagues at universities and research centers, seldom spending more than a month in one place. He carried all of his belongings in a shabby suitcase, and it was not unusual for him to show up on the doorstep of a famous mathematician with the greeting, "My brain is open." He would then spend a few days discussing a challenging math problem with his host or lecturing at the local university. "Another roof, another proof" was one of Erdös's favorite sayings. "Mathematicians on four continents have made Erdös's well-being their collective responsibility," John Tierney wrote in *Science* magazine. "They see it as their duty to mathematics." Working together, they ensured that he could continue his unusual—albeit intellectually productive—lifestyle and work habits. "He exists on a web of trust," said a colleague who drove him around during one trip. Although a visit from Erdös was demanding, mathematicians all over the world considered it a great honor to have him visit their institutions.

What little money Erdös earned, usually in the form of lecture fees, he either gave away or sent to a close friend, Ronald Graham of Bell Laboratories in New Jersey. Graham would deposit the money in a bank and send checks to anyone Erdös had borrowed from and to the various charitable causes Erdös supported. Like other mathematicians whom Erdös visited, Graham did everything for his friend when he came to town, driving him wherever he needed to go and taking care of his laundry and dental appointments. Erdös never had a driver's license, a checkbook, or a credit card. He once left for a trip to Japan without nothing more than $50 in cash. "There was no reason to worry," he explained. "I had friends everywhere along the way." But no one did more for Erdös than Ron Graham, who not only handled his finances but ended up building an addition onto his house in New Jersey so that Erdös would have his own bedroom when he came to visit.

It was obvious from the life he led that Erdös was completely dedicated to mathematics. Unlike other scientists, mathematicians require no labs or equipment to perform their work, so Erdős could carry around just a small suitcase of notes. He was ready to do math at any time and in any place. He would walk into a room and immediately start talking about whatever math problem was currently on his mind. Sometimes he offered cash rewards, ranging from $5 to $3000, for solutions to outstanding problems. When one of these problems was solved, he would have Ron Graham send a check to the person who came up with the solution.

One way of measuring a mathematician's accomplishment is to look at how many papers he or she has published in technical journals. An above-average mathematician might publish 20 articles, and a really great one might publish 50 articles in a lifetime. Paul Erdős published 50 papers in one year (1986), and more than 1,500 over the course of his lifetime. He worked with more than 500 different co-authors. In fact, collaborating with him was considered such a sign of prestige that mathematicians regularly referred to someone who had co-authored a paper with Erdős as having an "Erdős number" of one. If a mathematician published a paper with someone who had published a paper with Erdős, he or she was assigned an Erdős number of two, and so forth. Albert Einstein, the famous physicist, had an Erdős number of two.

> **" For Erdős, mathematics had its own kind of beauty. "It's like asking why Beethoven's Ninth Symphony is beautiful. If you don't see why, some-one can't tell you. I know numbers are beautiful. If they aren't beautiful, nothing is." "**

Erdős was once compared to a bee that makes plants flower by carrying pollen from one bloom to the next. He carried information and math problems from one university or research center to another, throughout the world. He spread his knowledge wherever he went and inspired both young and experienced mathematicians. One of his friends described him as "a one-man clearing house for information on the status of problems in his field."

Contributions to the Field of Mathematics

Erdős began his work in the field known as "number theory," which examines the properties of integers, or whole numbers. Erdős was particularly fascinated by what are known as "prime numbers." A number is prime if it can't be divided by any smaller number except one. The numbers 5, 7, and 11 are good examples. Prime numbers appear to be very simple, but all sorts of basic questions about them remain unanswered, even though they have been stud-

ied by mathematicians for hundreds of years. Erdös's first paper, written when he was only 18, proved that there is always at least one prime number between any integer and its double. For example, between 3 and its double, 6, lies the prime number 5. This had already been proved in the 19th century by a famous Russian mathematician, Pafnuty Lvovitch Chebyshev. Yet Erdös's proof was considered to be more "elegant," which in mathematical terms means more simple and concise. This little ditty was passed around to tell of Erdös's successful proof: "Chebyshev said it, and I say it again/ There is always a prime between n and $2n$."

After this early success in number theory, Erdös moved on to the field known as "combinatorics," which deals with combinations — with ways to classify and arrange the members of a set. Although it was an obscure field at the time he first became interested in it, combinatorics has turned out to be one of the fastest growing areas in mathematics. Among other things, it was fundamental to the development of computers — although Erdös himself never touched a computer and did all of his calculations either in his head or on paper. A typical problem involving combinatorics is what is called the "packing problem": how to arrange one-inch-square tiles so that they covered a parking lot as completely as possible without overlapping. The parking lot that he devised was 100,000.1 inches on each side, so the one-inch-square tiles could not cover it exactly. The easy and obvious way to arrange the tiles was in straight lines, in a graph pattern. But that would leave a 0.1 inch-wide uncovered strip along two sides. Altogether, that would leave a total of 20,000 square inches uncovered. So Erdös didn't take the easy and obvious approach. Instead, he came up with a paving scheme that turned the tiles at precise angles. Although his scheme left small gaps between the tiles, he had squeezed in an extra 6,000 tiles.

Erdös's brilliance lay in his ability to devise short, clever solutions based on insight rather than on pages and pages of complicated calculations. Once he was visiting a university in Texas and noticed a problem on the blackboard involving functional analysis, a field he knew almost nothing about. Two professors at the university were very proud of a 30-page solution to the problem that they had just devised. Erdös looked up at the blackboard and said, "What's that? Is it a problem?" When his host said "Yes," he squinted at the board for a few minutes, asked some questions about what the various symbols meant, and then wrote down a two-line solution.

For Erdös, mathematics had an aesthetic element. Beauty and insight are two of the qualities that he always looked for in his work. Yet he recognized that not everyone was capable of appreciating this type of beauty. "It's like asking why Beethoven's Ninth Symphony is beautiful," he once said. "If you don't see why, someone can't tell you. I *know* numbers are beautiful. If they aren't beautiful, nothing is."

One of Erdös's most renowned achievements is his proof of the "Prime Number Theorem," which he created with a colleague, Atle Selberg. The first proof of the Prime Number Theorem, which explains the pattern of distribution of prime numbers, dates back to 1896. The proof that Erdös and Selberg created in 1949 was considered superior to the earlier proof because it did not use the square root of -1, which the earlier proof had relied on. The square root of -1 is often referred to as an "imaginary number." By not using it, Erdös and Selberg's proof was considered "elementary" in the sense that it was more basic and pure. The two mathematicians agreed to publish their work back-to-back in the same professional journal, sharing the credit and explaining the contribution that each had made. But at the last minute, Selberg decided to race ahead and publish his proof first. He was awarded a major prize, but Erdös was not particularly upset by the incident. He never worried about competition with others in his field, only about solving problems that no one else had been able to solve.

Erdös and His Eccentricities

Friends who knew Erdös well called him "Uncle Paul" and often traded stories about his eccentricities. He always wore sandals, even when he went hiking in the Canadian Rockies. Any item of clothing that came in contact with his skin had to be made out of silk because of an undiagnosed skin condition that was irritated by other fabrics. He didn't like to touch people or be touched by them; he refused to shake hands or let people kiss him. He washed his hands dozens of times a day and was preoccupied with his own mortality. When he was still in his 50s, he started adding the initials P.G.O.M. (Poor Great Old Man) to his name. When he turned 60, he became P.G.O.M.L.D., with "L.D." standing for "Living Dead." At 65 he added A.D. (Archaeological Discovery) and at 70 he added another L.D. for "Legally Dead." At 75, the string of initials following his name became P.G.O.M.L.D.A.D.L.D.C.D. (Counts Dead).

Erdös also had his own unique vocabulary. He referred to God as "S.F." (the Supreme Fascist) because he knew all the answers but left mankind in the dark. Women were "bosses" and men were "slaves"; to be married was to be "captured," and children were "epsilons" (from the term used to describe very small quantities in mathematics). But he always regarded male and female mathematicians as equal, and he often entertained his friends' "epsilons" by performing tricks involving sleight-of-hand. When he said that someone "died," he meant that the person had stopped doing mathematics. And when he said someone had "left," he meant that the person had died.

Despite his eccentric behavior, Erdös was a very generous person. He was extremely kind to young mathematicians, lending them money if they needed it to pay their rent or buy a new car. When he won the Wolf Prize (the equivalent of the Nobel Prize in mathematics) he kept only about $700 of the $50,000 prize and gave the rest to relatives and to a scholarship fund he had established in Israel. Whenever he heard of a good cause, he would promptly make a donation. Erdös once gave away all the money he'd earned from a series of lectures in India to the widow of a well-known Indian mathematician.

The Perfect Death

After his mother's death in 1971, Erdös began taking amphetamines (commonly known as speed). The pills had originally been prescribed by a doctor to relieve the symptoms of depression, but he soon realized that with the help of medication, he could put in 19-hour work days. It wasn't long before he was addicted to the burst of energy the pills gave him, which he reinforced with strong coffee and caffeine tablets. Erdös once defined a mathematician as "a machine for turning coffee into theorems." Somehow his body managed to thrive on this punishing treatment.

Although his friends were constantly telling him to slow down, Erdös was still working 16-20 hours a day in his early 70s. "There is plenty of time to rest in the grave," he would tell them. His close friend Ron Graham once offered him $500 if he would stop taking speed for a month. Erdös accepted the challenge but warned Graham that he was "setting mathematics back a month." At the end of the month, he collected the $500 and immediately starting taking the pills again. As far as he was concerned, the experiment had proved that he was not an addict, but that he got less work done without the help of his "medication."

Erdös would often think about how he would like to die. He decided that the perfect death would occur just after he'd completed a lecture. Someone in the audience would raise a hand to ask an annoying question and Erdös would say, "I think I'll leave that to the next generation," and fall over dead. The

> "My mother said,
> 'Even you, Paul, can be in
> only one place at one time.'
> Maybe soon I will be relieved
> of this disadvantage.
> Maybe, once I've left [died],
> I'll be able to be in many
> places at the same time.
> Maybe then I'll be able
> to collaborate with
> Archimedes and Euclid."

circumstances surrounding his real death were not that far from this ideal. On September 20, 1996, while attending a mathematical conference in Warsaw, Poland, Erdös suffered a massive heart attack and died. He was 83. More than 500 people—many of them famous mathematicians—attended the memorial service held in his honor in Budapest. "You've heard about my mother's theorem?" Erdös once said about his own death. "My mother said, 'Even you, Paul, can be in only one place at one time.' Maybe soon I will be relieved of this disadvantage. Maybe, once I've left [died], I'll be able to be in many places at the same time. Maybe then I'll be able to collaborate with Archimedes and Euclid."

Erdös's Legacy

"The way Paul Erdös [conducted] his personal life," John Tierney wrote in *Science* magazine, "is exactly the way a pure mathematician conducts his work: with utter disregard for the real world." He eliminated all of the normal concerns of daily life—money, property, and family—so that he could devote all of his attention to math. He didn't worry about whether the problems he solved and the theorems he proved would have any practical results. All he cared about was finding the mathematical truth. His "driving force was his desire to understand and to know," said his longtime friend, Dr. Ron Graham. "You could think of it as Erdös's magnificent obsession. It determined everything in his life." That obsession made Erdös one of the greatest mathematicians of our time. "In our century, in which mathematics is so strongly dominated by 'theory doctors,'" Dr. Ernst Strauss wrote, "he has remained the prince of problem solvers and the absolute monarch of problem posers."

> "
>
> *According to John Tierney, "The way Paul Erdös [conducted] his personal life is exactly the way a pure mathematician conducts his work: with utter disregard for the real world."*
>
> "

HOME AND FAMILY

Erdös never married. His closest companion was his mother. From 1964 until her death in 1971, she traveled everywhere with him. They ate every meal together, and at night he held her hand until she fell asleep.

Although he was not interested in forming any other close relationships and was uncomfortable if someone even touched him, Erdös preferred the company of other mathematicians to being alone. His favorite activity was attending conferences, and he enjoyed being taken around by his hosts and eating dinner with their families.

HOBBIES AND OTHER INTERESTS

Erdös had very few interests outside of mathematics. He liked to play ping-pong, chess, and Go, and he occasionally listened to classical music on an old-fashioned transistor radio. But he had no time to waste on "frivolities" like reading novels or going to the movies. Once a colleague and his wife, who was a curator at the Museum of Modern Art in New York City, dragged Erdös to an exhibit of paintings by the French painter Henri Matisse. "We showed him Matisse," the colleague said, "but he would have nothing to do with it. After a few minutes, we ended up sitting in the sculpture garden doing mathematics."

WRITINGS

The Art of Counting, 1973

HONORS AND AWARDS

Cole Price (American Mathematical Society): 1951
National Academy of Sciences (Hungary): 1956
London Mathematical Society: 1973
National Academy of Sciences (US): 1979
Wolf Foundation Prize (co-winner): 1983
National Academy of Sciences (India): 1988
Royal Society (UK): 1989

FURTHER READING

Books

International Who's Who, 1996-97

Periodicals

Atlantic Monthly, Nov. 1987, p.60
Economist, Oct. 5, 1996, p.83
Los Angeles Times, Sep. 24, 1996, p.A18
Nature, Oct. 17, 1996, p.584
New York Times, Sep. 24, 1996, p.A1
New York Times Biographical Service, Sep. 1996, p.1394
Science, Apr. 8, 1977, p.144; Oct. 1984, p.40; Feb. 7, 1997, p.759
Time, Oct. 7, 1996, p.33
Times of London, Sep. 25, 1996, Features section
Washington Post, Sep. 24, 1996, p.B7; Sep. 27, 1996, p.A25

Other

"N Is a Number: A Portroit of Paul Erdös," 1993 (film documentary)

Walter Gilbert 1932-

American Molecular Biologist
Winner of the 1980 Nobel Prize in Chemistry

BIRTH

Walter Gilbert was born in Cambridge, Massachusetts, on March
21, 1932. He was one of two children born to Richard V. Gilbert
and Emma (Cohen) Gilbert, both of whom were of Russian
Jewish descent. His father was a professor of economics at
Harvard University until 1939, and his mother was a child psychologist who completed her studies at Radcliffe.

YOUTH

Gilbert's fascination with science was apparent from an early age. But although he was an extremely bright child, he did not perform well in school. During World War II, when his father worked in the Federal Office of Price Administration, the family moved to the area around Washington, D.C. Gilbert attended public schools in the city with little enthusiasm. He earned only average grades, and he often played hooky from school. At home, though, his parents encouraged his love for certain scientific subjects, such as astronomy and chemistry. As Gilbert grew older, he largely ignored the athletic activities of other children, turning instead to solitary scientific activities. Even as a youngster he constructed his own telescopes, grinding the mirrors for the telescope lenses himself, and he spent hours experimenting with his chemistry sets.

EDUCATION

Gilbert attended school at Sidwell Friends School, an exclusive private school in Washington, D.C. There, he emerged as an outstanding science student armed with a seemingly unquenchable thirst to increase his knowledge in all areas of science. He later admitted that "I spent my senior year [of high school] reading about nuclear physics in the Library of Congress." Gilbert graduated from Sidwell Friends School in 1949.

"I spent my senior year [of high school] reading about nuclear physics in the Library of Congress."

Gilbert entered Harvard University in 1949 as a chemistry and physics major. He graduated in 1953 summa cum laude (with the highest honors). He remained at Harvard to obtain his master's degree in physics in 1954. He then left for England to study theoretical physics at Cambridge University.

At Cambridge Gilbert met a number of brilliant scientists who encouraged his interest in scientific research. He studied theoretical physics under Abdus Salam, who later became a Nobel laureate. Gilbert also met biologist James D. Watson and physicist Francis Crick, who had gained worldwide fame for their discovery of the structure of DNA (deoxyribonucleic acid), the molecule in every cell that holds the information necessary for that cell to reproduce and to pass on genetic information.

Gilbert graduated from Cambridge in 1957 with a doctoral degree (Ph.D.) in mathematics. In his doctoral thesis, he used complex mathematical formulas to predict the behavior of elementary particles after experimental scattering. Gilbert then returned to Harvard University as a National Science Foundation postdoctoral fellow in physics.

CAREER HIGHLIGHTS

Turning to Molecular Biology

It is quite unusual for a scientist trained in one specialized area to jump into another highly technical area, but Gilbert successfully made such a leap. By 1959 Gilbert had been named an assistant professor of physics at Harvard, but a year later he renewed his acquaintance with Watson, who was now at Harvard. Watson was attempting to isolate the molecule that in effect "carries instructions" from DNA to the ribosomes, the structures within the cell where proteins are made. This molecule, which exists for only a short time, is called mRNA, or messenger ribonucleic acid.

Fascinated with the mRNA studies and excited by Watson's insights, Gilbert joined Watson's team. By doing so, Gilbert jumped out of the world of physics and into the newly emerging world of molecular biology, the study of how cells reproduce and manufacture life-sustaining substances.

For years, scientists had known that it is DNA that holds the master plan of the inner life of the cell. But they did not understand *how* DNA functioned. It was the discovery of the structure of DNA by Watson and Crick that ushered in the new branch of science called molecular biology. This new frontier in biological research held enormous implications for the future, as scientists sought to gain a complete understanding of DNA and its functions.

DNA resides in the nucleus of every cell of all living forms, whether plant or animal. It contains the elements that differentiate a squash from a tomato or a dog from a human. It is composed of four different kinds of units that are commonly known as bases. These DNA bases, which can be arranged in an almost infinite variety of sequences, determine the nature of cells. In addition, the DNA in each cell makes the cell act in a particular way. A skin cell, for instance, "knows" it is a skin cell, and directs the manufacture of the proteins necessary for that function, while DNA in a bone cell makes different proteins specifically intended for that cell's bone-building function.

Gilbert's DNA Research

In 1964, after only five years at Harvard, Gilbert became an associate professor of biophysics, and in 1968 he became a full professor of biochemistry. Throughout the 1960s, Gilbert and others tried to understand the process whereby DNA issues instructions for the cell to produce a specific protein. As part of the Watson research team that successfully isolated the first mRNA,

Gilbert demonstrated that a single strand of this messenger molecule could have a simultaneous effect on more than one ribosome.

Once these facts were well-proven and accepted, the next big quest was to gain an understanding of how a gene "turns on" and "turns off." Scientists recognized that even though cells in a body contained the same genetic information, some genes within those cells were turned "on," while others were turned "off." But the genes that were "on" and "off" varied from cell to cell, in accordance with their needs. Researchers all over the world were determined to figure out how this "on-off" switch worked.

By the late 1960s, Gilbert was hot on the trail that had been blazed by two French geneticists, François Jacob and Jacques Monod. These two scientists had proposed the existence of a repressor molecule that prevented the activity of particular genes under certain conditions. Such a theory would explain how a red blood cell could make hemoglobin but not insulin, and how a cell in the pancreas might make insulin but not hemoglobin.

Gilbert himself was excited by the new challenge of launching a company. "I'm driven by . . . an intense curiosity. I love new things, new ideas, new facts. It goes along with tremendous impatience."

Gilbert launched his own tests, using a common intestinal bacteria known as *Escherichia coli*, or *E. coli*, as his model. The scientist chose bacterium for his experiments because of its simple genetic structure.

Gilbert knew that in the presence of lactose, a sugar found in milk, *E. coli* produces an enzyme that further breaks down the sugar. But since this enzyme was produced only when the bacterium was in milk, Gilbert hypothesized that the DNA of *E. coli* contained a *lac* (for lactose) repressor molecule that attaches to that critical part of the gene. When lactose is present, the repressor molecule becomes detached from the DNA strand and the lac operator region then sends an mRNA to produce the lactose-digesting enzyme. Gilbert found and identified the lac repressor and confirmed the process whereby a gene "turns on and off." He later located the region on the *E. coli* DNA known as the lac operator.

During the 1970s, Gilbert continued on the path to identifying regions of DNA that were responsible for certain functions. This process is known as "sequencing." It involves treating DNA with chemical compounds that are able to break the DNA into strands of known length and then separating these strands even further by using an electric field in a special gel. The chem-

Dr. Gilbert and co-worker, Professor Jack Strominger celebrate the announcement of his sharing of the 1980 Nobel Prize for chemistry

ical code of DNA can then be read after X-ray exposure. This technique proved to be an extremely fast and efficient way to "read" DNA.

Once it was known how to sequence portions of DNA, it was believed that DNA's double-helix structure could then be manipulated to produce any one of the thousands of proteins encoded in the DNA. Experiments confirmed this theory, and excited researchers proclaimed that this knowledge might enable them to manufacture human proteins to treat various genetic diseases.

Gilbert was one of the pioneers in this new field, known as genetic engineering. By 1976, Gilbert and several other Harvard researchers were engaged in head-to-head competition with other laboratories across the country to produce human insulin in this manner. Other proteins were also touted as materials that could be mass-produced via genetic engineering, including interferon (used to treat cancer) and human growth hormone (used to stimulate growth).

Producing human proteins was not a new concept. It had even been achieved in the past, although researchers had experienced many problems. But Gilbert and other supporters of genetic engineering argued that new knowledge and technology could revolutionize production of important proteins. Even opponents of the new technology admitted that science had reached a new frontier in the study of molecular biology.

Biogen

In 1978 Gilbert was asked to head up a new biotechnology company called Biogen, with headquarters in Geneva, Switzerland, and Cambridge, Massachusetts. For the first few years, he continued his work at Harvard at the same time. At first Gilbert was reluctant to venture into business. To preserve the purity of research, the world of academics had traditionally distanced itself from the world of money. In the growth of the biotechnology industry, the two worlds began a new—and often uneasy—alliance. As Gilbert once explained, he and his academic colleagues had a desire "to do something socially useful, wanting to create an industrial structure, wanting to make something grow, wanting to make money. Although the desire to make money is not that high, generally, in scientists."

Gilbert was admired for his passion and his intellect, and many people thought he was the perfect choice to lead Biogen. As one observer noted, Gilbert "has the knack of peering over the scientific horizon and spotting distant but attainable scientific destinations—and intuiting the intermediate steps to get there." Gilbert himself was excited by the new challenge of launching a company. "I'm driven by . . . an intense curiosity," he said. "I love new things, new ideas, new facts. It goes along with tremendous impatience."

Nobel Prize

In 1980 Gilbert and Frederick Sanger, a professor at Cambridge University, were jointly awarded the Nobel Prize for Chemistry for the chemical methods of gene sequencing they had discovered separately in the 1970s. Working independently, they had each developed a method for rapidly determining the exact chemical makeup for large pieces of DNA. According to the Nobel committee, their contributions "have to a considerable degree increased our knowledge of the way in which DNA, as the carrier of genetic traits, governs the chemical machinery of the cell." Gilbert said that he was "delighted, pleased, and tremendously honored" to share this prize.

Gilbert's Nobel Prize added further luster to Biogen's image, and a year later Gilbert was named chief executive officer of the company. His new responsibilities convinced him to take a leave of absence from Harvard so he could devote all his energies to making Biogen succeed.

Over the next several years, the company posted mixed results in its efforts to translate biotechnology advances into profits. By 1980 Biogen was manufacturing interferon, a product that was expected to provide a therapeutic breakthrough in the fight against cancer. Biogen grew rapidly. When it became a publicly held company in 1983, its stock sold for $23 a share. But interferon did not prove to be a miracle cure, and Gilbert came under increasing criticism for the company's sizable research expenditures and meager earnings.

When Gilbert won the Nobel Prize in 1980, the Nobel committee said that his work has "increased our knowledge of the way in which DNA, as the carrier of genetic traits, governs the chemical machinery of the cell."

Gilbert's relationship with other company executives deteriorated, and investors began to grumble about Biogen's performance and Gilbert's management style. One of the company founders argued that the scientist was "determined to make Biogen a fantastically large pharmaceutical company. And the way he's going at it, either that's going to happen or the company's going to run out of money. He's like an old New England mariner steering his ship through a storm. Come hell or high water, he's going to hold his course."

In late 1984 Biogen's stock dropped to $5 a share, and Gilbert was asked to resign from the company. He left in December 1984 and returned to the Harvard faculty, where he later reflected on his years at Biogen: "That whole period was a distraction from my deeper interests in science, which are ultimately not the same as the company's."

Back at Harvard, Gilbert's academic career soared. In 1986 Gilbert was named the H.H. Timken professor of science. A year later, he was named chairman of the Department of Cellular and Developmental Biology and assumed the title of Carl M. Loeb University Professor.

Human Genome Project

As the 1980s unfolded, Gilbert became convinced that future growth in molecular biology depended on gaining a greater understanding of individual genes. Some researchers had begun to argue in favor of a project that would map out the entire human genetic map by determining the arrangement of the estimated 100,000 genes that make up the human genome (a complete set of chromosomes). Proponents insisted that such knowledge would have far-reaching implications for the future of medicine and the knowledge of how we, as a biological species, operate. The supporters of this project, including Gilbert, claimed that thorough DNA mapping would accelerate research into cures for Down's syndrome, cystic fibrosis, and many other hereditary diseases.

The federal government was initially undecided about whether it should commit money to the project, so Gilbert tried to establish a private business to undertake the cost of the research. In 1987 he announced that he intended to raise $10 million to form the company, which he called the Genome Corporation. "I very much think of myself as an entrepreneur," he said. "What I enjoy most is the innovative moment. To see a company built out of an idea is very satisfying and gratifying."

A short time later, however, the U.S. government decided that the project was worthwhile. It offered to provide financial support to Gilbert's company, as long as it operated under the direction and control of the National Institutes of Health Center for Human Genome Research. Gilbert objected to the terms, though, and after thinking about the demands of the project, decided that he would not be able to get the Genome Corporation off the ground.

The Human Genome Research Project, under the direction of Dr. Francis Collins of the University of Michigan, continues to be funded by the federal government as an extension of the National Institutes of Health. Even supporters admit that it will require billions of dollars to map the entire human DNA, and some people do not think the project is worth the price. Others have doubts about the ethics of the project. They question who will own this genetic information — the individual, or the medical community, or the insurance companies? How will such information remain private? And could the information gained be used for unethical purposes — for example, to deny employment or insurance coverage to someone with a genetic condition, or to do cloning against their will. Gilbert, though, remains confident. He is certain that the project, when completed, will revolutionize the way scientists conduct their research.

Recent Projects

Recently, Gilbert started working as chairman of a new biotechnology company called NetGenics. This new company creates computer software that is used by prescription drug companies. These drug companies now work with huge libraries of genetic information, searching through DNA sequences to determine which might help them develop new drugs. It's a huge task to sort through all the data. This has given rise to a new field, called bioinformatics, to help scientists with this sorting process. NetGenics is part of this bioinformatics field. It makes computer software that allows scientists to manipulate DNA information more easily and also allows team members working in different labs to share their work on computer.

—— " ——

"I very much think of myself as an entrepreneur. What I enjoy most is the innovative moment. To see a company built out of an idea is very satisfying and gratifying."

—— " ——

In addition, Gilbert has been studying the origin of genes. He and his team of fellow researchers at Harvard University have used extensive computer and statistical analyses to try to understand what the first genes were like when life first formed over three billion years ago. They hope to make sense of what Gilbert has called "one of the major unsolved mysteries of the basis of life": why DNA contains long stretches of useless, nonsense material (which he calls exons). "His theory is an effort to figure out how, in the primordial waters where life began, the earliest genes were assembled," Philip J. Hilts explained in the *New York Times.* It is an incredibly difficult question, and one that few scientists are willing to tackle. As Dr. Philip Sharp of the Massachusetts Institute of Technology noted, "Yes, it is very difficult. It may even be unsolvable. That won't stop Wally Gilbert, of course."

HOBBIES AND OTHER INTERESTS

Gilbert brings a sense of passion to whatever he does. Some of his recent pursuits include the study of patent law, Chinese cooking, piano, and collecting ancient Greek statues.

MARRIAGE AND FAMILY

Walter Gilbert, known to friends and family as "Wally," married Celia Stone, a poet, in December 1953. They have two children, John Richard and Kate, and live in the Cambridge, Massachusetts, area.

HONORS AND AWARDS

United States Steel Foundation Award (National Academy of Sciences): 1968
Elected to American Academy of Arts and Sciences: 1968

Ledlie Prize (Harvard University): 1969

Elected to National Academy of Sciences: 1976

Prix Charles-Leopold Mayer (Institut de France): 1977

Warren Triennial Prize (Massachusetts General Hospital): 1977

Louis and Bert Freedman Award (New York Academy of Sciences): 1977

Harrison Howe Award (Rochester branch of American Chemical Society): 1978

Albert Lasker Basic Medical Research Award (Albert and Mary Lasker Foundation): 1979

Gairdner Foundation Award: 1979

Louisa Gross Horwitz Prize (Columbia University): 1979

Herbert A. Sober Memorial Award (American Society of Biological Chemists): 1980

Nobel Prize for Chemistry: 1980 (joint prize, with Frederick Sanger), "for their contributions concerning the determination of base sequences in nucleic acids"

Elected to British Royal Society: 1987

New England Entrepreneur of the Year Award: 1991

FURTHER READING

Books

Encyclopedia Britannica, 1995

Hall, Stephen. *Invisible Frontiers,* 1987

Who's Who in America, 1994

Periodicals

Boston Magazine, May 1990, p.113; Jan. 1997, p.44

Business Week, Jan. 7, 1985, p.46; Apr. 27, 1987, p.116

Current Biography Yearbook 1992

Discover, Jan. 1988, p.85

Fortune, Nov. 9, 1987, p.142

Health, July/Aug. 1996, p.32

New York Times, Oct. 15, 1980, p.A1 and A16; Nov. 12, 1996, p.C1

New York Times Magazine, Dec. 13, 1987, p.44

Omni, Nov. 1992, p.91

Science, Nov. 21, 1980, p.887; Feb. 1984, p.42; Aug. 9, 1991, p.677

Science '85, Feb. 1985, p.42

Scientific American, Mar. 1991, p.27

Time, Oct. 27, 1980, p.76

ADDRESS

Biological Laboratories
Harvard University
16 Divinity Avenue
Cambridge, MA 02138-2020

WORLD WIDE WEB SITE

http://golgi.harvard.edu/gilbert.html

Stephen Jay Gould 1941-
American Paleontologist, Geologist, and Essayist
Theorist on Evolutionary Biology

BIRTH

Stephen Jay Gould was born in New York City, New York, on September 10, 1941. His parents were Eleanor (Rosenberg) Gould and Leonard Gould, a court stenographer for the Queens County Supreme Court. Stephen had one younger brother, Peter.

YOUTH

Gould grew up in a lower middle class neighborhood in Queens, a borough of New York City. Like many kids, he liked to think about what he wanted to do with his life when he grew up. But unlike most kids, Gould actually made up his mind at a very young age. It was a trip to the Hall of Dinosaurs in the American Museum of Natural History that helped him decide. "When I was four I wanted to be a garbage man. I loved the rattling of the cans and the whir of the compressor: I thought that all of New York's trash might be squeezed into a single, capacious truck. Then, when I was five, my father took me to see the *Tyrannosaurus* at the American Museum of Natural History. As we stood in front of the beast, a man sneezed," Gould recounts. He was absolutely terrified, sure the dinosaur skeleton was coming to life. "But the great animal stood immobile in all its bony grandeur, and as we left, I announced that I would be a paleontologist when I grew up." As Gould now recalls, "I had no idea there were such things—I was awestruck."

Leonard Gould, Stephen's father, was a self-taught man, an amateur naturalist, and a Marxist. He and Eleanor Gould, Stephen's mother, supported and encouraged their son's interests. "At five or six," Eleanor recalls, "he'd go to the beach and classify shells into categories—regular, extraordinary, and unusual. And he had lots of collections: baseball cards, cigarette packages. I'd accommodate him by smoking a different brand every time." Each summer, the family would visit abandoned rock quarries and dry river beds, looking for dinosaur bones. He never found any, although he collected boxes full of marine fossils. According to Stephen, "[The] family had a respect for learning. Of course, it was absolutely necessary in terms of kiddie culture to claim that you didn't like school, but I always loved it."

> ———— " ————
>
> *"If you were interested in dinosaurs, you were seen as a nerd on the school playground. . . . I think many scientific careers are squelched on the playgrounds of [elementary schools]. There are always some really committed people, like me as a kid, who take the teasing, but many people who would have been very good scientists were just permanently derailed."*
>
> ———— " ————

At that time there wasn't much interest in dinosaurs, the way there is today. As Gould recalls, his interest singled him out as a misfit. In fact, he was teased as a kid—he was called "fossil face" by the other kids at school. "There were no films or lunch boxes or pencils emblazoned with dinosaurs," Gould recalls. "If you were interested in dinosaurs, you were seen as a nerd on the school playground. . . . I think many scientific careers are squelched on the playgrounds of [elementary schools]. There are always some really committed people, like me as a kid, who take the teasing, but many people who would have been very good scientists were just permanently derailed."

EDUCATION

Gould attended Jamaica High School in Queens, New York, graduating in about 1959. He spent the summer after graduation at the University of Colorado before continuing his studies at Antioch College, a small, prestigious liberal arts college in Yellow Springs, Ohio. He took classes in philosophy, biology, and geology. He was particularly impressed with a professor's collection of snail fossils from Bermuda. Gould earned a bachelor of arts (B.A.) degree from Antioch in 1963. He gives Antioch a lot of the credit for his development as a scientist and thinker.

Gould's interests and career plans never wavered while he was in school, as he explains here. "I always felt that it [was very comforting to have a clear sense of direction], particularly being in college in tumultuous times, in the '60s, with so many friends who were being buffeted, mostly by political issues. . . . [At Antioch], my various left-wing friends couldn't understand why someone of similar politics would have an interest in being a paleontologist. And yet it was wonderfully comforting: I really did know what I wanted to do as a lifetime profession."

Gould went on to do graduate work in paleontology at Columbia University in New York City. He was especially drawn there by the opportunity to work at the Museum of Natural History, which had so impressed him as a child. At Columbia, he continued his study of the Bermuda snail fossils that had intrigued him at Antioch. Gould earned his Ph.D. (doctoral degree) in paleontology from Columbia in 1967.

FIRST JOBS

Gould was still doing graduate work at Columbia in 1966 when he got his first professional job—teaching at Antioch College. The following year, after he earned his Ph.D., he was immediately hired by Harvard University. He started as an assistant professor of geology at Harvard in 1967, advanced to associate professor in 1971, and became a full professor in 1973. In addition, he has served as curator of invertebrate paleontology at Harvard's Museum of Comparative Zoology.

CAREER HIGHLIGHTS

For 30 years, Gould has been sharing his love of paleontology with the world. He is an extremely popular teacher at Harvard, where his classes in geology, biology, and the history of science fill up quickly. Indeed, his contagious enthusiasm for his subject and his lively lecturing style have made his classes so popular that about 800 students often try to enroll in a class that only accepts 300. Gould is also a prolific science writer who is well known in both the scientific community and the general public. Among scientists, he is known for his theoretical writings on evolution and for his expertise on the Cerion snail from the West Indies. Among the general public, Gould is known for his engaging and readable science essays in *Natural History* magazine and in book form.

Getting Started in Field Research

Gould started out his career in the late 1960s as a professor at Harvard. Yet he didn't limit himself to teaching; as he explains here, "Every natural historian has to have a focus of empirical expertise." Gould's area of expertise is the Cerion snail, a small land snail that grows to about four centimeters. Here, he explains how he decided to study this snail. "I decided that I wanted to study evolutionary pattern in a statistical way, and you can't do that with dinosaurs. There are only two Tyrannosaurus skeletons in the entire world, so you could not do a rigorous study of rates of evolution in tyrannosaurs. If you want to study rates and patterns, you need material that comes in thousands rather than handsful as specimens. That meant invertebrates rather than vertebrates. Snails suit my own interest because I'm concerned with the relationship between growth and evolution, and snails preserve in their shells the record of their entire growth from babyhood to adult. Most organisms don't."

Gould has taken many trips to the West Indies to do field research. Working with a biologist, he would crawl on his hands and knees along the beaches of the Bahamas and collect examples of the various species of the Cerion snail. Returning to Harvard, he would sort and classify the snails, writing up his findings in scientific journals. These experiences — combining teaching at a university with doing original research and writing scientific papers — are fairly typical for an academic working in a scientific field.

Evolution and the Theory of Punctuated Equilibrium

In addition to his interest in the Cerion snail, Gould was always fascinated by evolutionary theory. In 1972, he and fellow paleontologist Niles Eldredge published a scientific paper that challenged the way many people view the process of evolution. They advanced a theory they called "punctuated equilibrium" to address some aspects of the methods of evolutionary change.

Evolutionary theory was first developed by Charles Darwin in his seminal book, *Origin of Species* (1859). Darwin envisioned evolution as a slow, gradual process of continuous transformations, from simple beginnings to more complex life forms. He argued that a species changes in very small increments through natural selection, or survival of the fittest, which ensures the survival of individuals or groups that adapt best to the environment. According to

Darwin, the evolution of a species, with each of its individual small changes, could be traced on a continuum stretching through millions of years.

Fossils in the earth's surface offer documentary proof of the existence of earlier life forms. According to Darwin's theory, there should be fossils to document the transitional steps in the evolution of various species. But few of these transitional fossils can be found; in fact, the fossil record does not support Darwin's view of evolution as gradual. What the fossil record shows, instead, is long periods of stability within a species, interrupted by sudden changes. Darwin's adherents argue that that is not a refutation of the theory but a reflection of the incompleteness of the fossil record, which has preserved only a small fraction of organisms throughout time.

But Gould and Eldredge took a different approach. They developed a theory they called punctuated equilibrium — known as "punk eke" by its admirers, and "evolution by jerks" by its detractors. While they agreed with the broad outlines of Darwin's theory of evolution, they suggested some changes in method. They suggested accepting the fossil record as is. What it shows, in their view, is that evolution occurs in unpredictable fits and starts. Most species remain stable and unchanged throughout most of their history, and most changes occur rapidly in geologic time—over the course of perhaps 50,000 years. These changes occur in small, isolated populations, which may explain why they so rarely appear in fossils. New species seem to split off at random from existing ones, and old species become extinct, all for reasons that are not well understood. This has profound implications for humans, of course, as Gould explains here. "We're not just evolving slowly," he says, "for all practical purposes we're not evolving at all. There's no reason to think we're going to get bigger brains or smaller toes or whatever—we are what we are."

Becoming an Essayist

Gould became an essayist quite by chance. In 1973, he got a call from Alan Ternes, the editor of *Natural History*, a science magazine for general readers that is published by the American Museum of Natural History in New York City. Ternes asked Gould if he would like to write a few columns. Although he had only written technical scientific papers up until that point, Gould agreed. In 1974 he began writing a monthly column called "This View of Life," and he has written a column every single month since then—over 250 pieces so far. Many of these essays were later collected and republished in book form. Gould has won many scientific and literary awards for his work, including a MacArthur Foundation award in 1981 that paid him over $38,000 annually for five years.

—————— " ——————

"[There] are about half a dozen scientific subjects that are immensely intriguing to people because they deal with fundamental issues that disturb us and cause us to wonder. Evolution is one of those subjects. It attempts, insofar as science can, to answer the questions of what our life means, and why we are here, and where we came from, and who we are related to, and what has happened through time, and what has been the history of this planet. These are questions that all thinking people have to ponder."

—————— " ——————

In these writings, Gould has reached a huge popular audience. Readers enjoy his elegant, lively style, graceful language, and ability to explain scientific methodology and theory in a way that is clear without being simplistic. As Wendy Smith wrote in *Publishers Weekly*, "Gould has used his columns for *Natural History* [collected in such volumes as *Ever Since Darwin*, *The Panda's Thumb*, *Hen's Teeth and Horse's Toes*, and *The Flamingo's Smile*]. . . to illuminate and demystify the scientific method—in the process giving the lay reader a witty, passionate survey in the history of science. . . . His chatty, colloquial prose reaches out to the general reader, striving to make even the most technical issues explicable, and openly avowing his own personal convictions so that the reader, agreeing or disagreeing, always knows where Gould stands."

Gould has a particular talent for making analogies between seemingly unrelated ideas. "The thing I do well is to see connections among things," he says. "I don't know why. I always just thought everybody made 100 references to this poem or that baseball game during any conversation. . . . I'm lousy at other things. I'm not good at logical sequencing or analysis. I see these interconnections, sometimes forced to be sure, but this works very well in the essay format."

Gould's curiosity and broad range of interests have led him to explore a varied range of topics in his writings. Using examples from the natural world, he has covered the basic principles of the Darwinian theory of evolution and explored its implications. For example, he once wrote about the panda's thumb, which it uses to peel leaves from bamboo shoots. The development of a thumb on the panda, a member of the bear family, allowed it to evolve from a meat-eating animal to one that can eat plants. But as he explained, it's not really a thumb at all, but instead an extension of the wrist bone. It's an inelegant solution, to be sure, but one that works beautifully for the panda. To Gould, it's inconceivable that a divine creator would devise such an arrangement. He considers it, instead, one more piece of evidence for evolution.

Scientific Theory Collides with the Political and Social Climate

Over the years, Gould has often presented arguments on political and social issues. He firmly believes that scientific thought rises out of a particular social climate — scientists are inevitably influenced by the times in which they live, and their prejudices and assumptions can influence their findings in the laboratory and in the field. And of course, sometimes they're wrong. He is a leader in the fight against sociobiology, a theory that says that human traits result from genetics and evolution. By implication, human potential is largely determined by an individual's genetic makeup. This gives rise to biological determinism, which he defines as "a theory of limits. It takes the current status of groups as a measure of where they should and must be (even while it allows some rare individuals to rise as a consequence of their fortunate biology)." Supporters of biological determinism argue that human potential is determined by genetics rather than environment, which Gould disputes. "Think of Cro-Magnon people 50,000 years ago," he says. "They were us. There's no difference in the brain capacity and intellectual abilities. What's happened is all cultural evolution."

Many of his writings review the history of science to expose such attitudes. In his 1981 volume *The Mismeasure of Man*, a full-length volume devoted to a single subject, Gould focuses on just one aspect of biological determinism. He analyzes scientists' ways of measuring intelligence through the ages and their efforts to rank people by intelligence. "This book," Gould writes, "is about the abstraction of intelligence as a single entity, its location within the brain, its quantification as one number for each individual, and the use of these numbers to rank people in a single series of worthiness, invariably to find that oppressed or disadvantaged groups — races, classes, or sexes — are innately inferior and deserve their status." He attacks in equal measure both the views of earlier scientists who believed that intelligence can be measured through craniometry, the science of measuring skulls, as well as the views of modern scientists who believe that intelligence can be measured by aptitude testing. He reserves his most scathing attacks for the use of intelligence testing to justify racist and sexist attitudes and behavior.

Another social and political issue that is important to Gould is that of evolution vs. creationism. He opposes the views of creationists, fundamentalist Christians who believe in a literal interpretation of the Bible story of creation. Many creationists have opposed the teaching of evolution in the schools and have demanded equal time for their views. In 1981, Gould was a star witness in a trial in Little Rock, Arkansas. This court case was designed to challenge a state law that required that public schools give a balanced treatment of "creation science" and "evolution science." Gould testified that creationism is refuted by all scientific evidence and does not deserve to be considered science. The end result of the trial was that creationism was considered a religion, not a science. Because the U.S. Constitution guarantees the separation of church and state, religion can not be taught in the public schools. The Arkansas state law was thus struck down.

A Diagnosis of Cancer

In 1982, Gould was having a regular checkup with his doctor when he asked to have a prostate exam. The doctor told him that the exam was unnecessary for a man of Gould's age, but agreed to do it anyway. The doctor found a lump that turned out to be mesothelioma, a form of cancer that is related to exposure to asbestos. At first, the doctor was rather vague about the prognosis for the disease. When Gould went to the Harvard library to read up on the medical literature, he understood why. Half of the people with mesothelioma live for only eight months after it is detected. Survival rates are so low because this type of cancer usually remains undetected until it's too late. For Gould, it was an extremely lucky fluke that his cancer was caught so early.

Gould was determined to improve his odds. He withstood an aggressive treatment regime of surgery, chemotherapy, and radiation that made him extremely ill. He had to cancel a trip to the Bahamas to do some field work, although he continued to teach and to write his column for *Natural History*

magazine, never missing a month. Gould was one of the lucky ones — there has been no recurrence of the cancer to date. After this experience, he continued his work with renewed enthusiasm and a subtle shift in his attitude toward life. "In my youth I was very much into this macho idea of science as rigid, hard, quantifiable," he once said. "Now I'm more interested in the beautiful and quirky contingencies that nature often takes."

Refining His Ideas on Evolution

Throughout his years of writing, Gould has continued to refine his view of evolution. In his essays and in several book-length studies, Gould has challenged the typical view of evolution, and humanity's role in it. "It is a picture we all carry around in our heads," Jerry Adler explained in *Newsweek* magazine, "the most powerful icon of the Age of Secular Humanism: the line of ascent of Man. It begins with bacteria, just barely across the threshold of life, a tenuous scum on primeval seas. Then, climbing the ladder of complexity that inexorably leads to [intelligent humans]: protozoa, invertebrates, the fishes and early reptiles. Followed by the first mammals, which knocked off the dinosaurs, the early primates and their hominid descendants huddled around a cave fire. Three billion years of progress directed toward the production of Man, a creature capable of abstract thought. . . . [Why] do we imagine that we are the necessary product and end of this titanic struggle toward perfection?"

This is the main theme of many of Gould's recent writings on evolutionary theory. He has questioned the common view that evolution is a progression from primitive life forms toward more complex, better adapted, superior animals — toward humans, in fact. In his view, there is nothing inherent in evolution that directed it toward the creation of humans, and nothing predestined about our current pre-eminence on earth. There is no grand plan involved in natural selection; it is chaotic, and much happens by chance.

Gould explicated this view in detail in one of his most important works, *Wonderful Life: The Burgess Shale and the Nature of History* (1989), a booklength analysis of fossils from a site in British Columbia. Considered the most important fossil find in the history of paleontology, the Burgess Shale was discovered in 1909. Much of the fossil record was misinterpreted at first, but it has been reexamined by several scientists in recent years. The Burgess Shale is a slab of exposed rock that contains a fossil bed with some of the world's most unusual fossils, which were created by a catastrophic event half a billion years ago. The variety of fossils there has led to a rethinking of evolutionary theory.

The Darwinian view is that evolution progressed from a few simple life forms to the many complex forms of today's varied and specialized creatures. Yet the Burgess Shale clearly shows an astonishing diversity of life forms from 500 million years ago, which contradicts Darwin's theory. Also, many of these forms have become extinct. Why did some survive while others perished? A large element of luck seems to be involved. And, in fact, it was just luck that our earliest ancestors weren't wiped out. There was nothing guaranteed about the emergence of humanity—some completely different life forms might have emerged. Gould's view is summarized here by Wendy Smith. "Natural history is, in fact, a messy chaotic process punctuated by mass extinctions that wiped out some well-adapted and highly successful species (like those in the Burgess Shale) for no apparent reason. Humans are not the be-all and end-all of creation. The basic idea that Gould is trying to get across in *Wonderful Life* is that of contingency, the understanding that the evolution of life was determined in part by chance events."

Response to His Work

Gould's ideas about evolution, particularly his theory of punctuated equilibrium, have been controversial among some scientists. Many have objected because he does not answer a crucial question in evolutionary theory: how and why a new species develops. Gould has inspired a mixed response in the scientific community. Some have argued that his work is derivative and unoriginal. They believe that fame and popularity are more important to him than his scientific work. Others have disparaged him for writing for the general public, rather than a strictly scientific audience. Yet others have praised his theoretical work as breakthroughs and lauded his ability to inform and educate the general reader through his essays. In all, his work has gained widespread acceptance by scientists over the years.

Current Activities

Gould now splits his time between Massachusetts and New York, working part of the year as a professor at Harvard and part of the year as a visiting professor at New York University. In addition, he has continued to write essays for *Natural History* magazine and to publish his essays in collections. His two most recent essay collections are *Dinosaur in a Haystack: Reflections in Natural History* (1995) and *Full House: The Spread of Excellence from Plato to Darwin* (1996). In the essays collected here, he continues to explore the principles of evolution with the same standards of readability and scientific integrity that exist in all his work. Yet in 1996, Gould wrote that he would end his long run of essays in *Natural History* magazine in January 2001. "I love doing this monthly work, but all good things must end," he explained.

But Gould doesn't plan to stop writing. His most recent publication is *Questioning the Millennium: A Rationalist's Guide to a Precisely Arbitrary Countdown* (1997). In this volume, he examines what the millennium is, questions when it begins, theorizes about why people are so intrigued by the calendar, and marvels, overall, at the human need to impose order on the chaos of the universe. He has also been working for over ten years on a massive treatise called *The Structure of Evolutionary*

Theory. At last count, the manuscript contained over 1,000 pages. But Gould doesn't seem concerned about losing interest in his subject. "Oh, evolutionary theory is so expansive," he says, "there's enough there to keep anyone going for a lifetime."

After 30 years, in fact, the subject of evolution continues to fascinate him. "[There] are about half a dozen scientific subjects," Gould says, "that are immensely intriguing to people because they deal with fundamental issues that disturb us and cause us to wonder. Evolution is one of those subjects. It attempts, insofar as science can, to answer the questions of what our life means, and why we are here, and where we came from, and who we are related to, and what has happened through time, and what has been the history of this planet. These are questions that all thinking people have to ponder."

MARRIAGE AND FAMILY

Gould is a very private person. He refuses to divulge much information about his personal life and has taken great pains to protect his family's privacy. Still, some facts are known. Gould has been married twice. His first wife was Deborah Lee, an artist and writer whom he met at Antioch College. They were married in October 1965 and had two sons, Jesse and Ethan. One of his sons is learning disabled. Gould and his wife were divorced after about 30 years of marriage.

In about 1996, Gould married Rhonda Roland Shearer, a painter, sculptor, and writer. They split their time between Massachusetts and New York City, where Shearer has lived. They recently remodeled a 4,200-square-foot loft in the Soho district, an artsy area of Manhattan. There, they created a huge loft that includes spacious living quarters, separate libraries for each of them, and an art studio for Shearer.

FAVORITE BOOKS

Here, Gould discusses the writers whose works he enjoys rereading. "I love to reread the three greatest scientific essayists in the English language: T.H. Huxley, J.B.S. Haldane, and P.B. Medawar. Though spanning a century, they share many characteristics. All were (or are, in Sir Peter Medawar's case) exemplary research scientists, not commentators from the outside world of journalism. All write about the simplest things and draw from them a universe of implications. . . . All maintain an unflinching commitment to rationality amid the soft attractions of an uncritical mysticism. . . . All demonstrate a deep commitment to the demystification of science by cutting through jargon: they show by example rather than exhortation that the most complex concepts can be rendered intelligible to everyone and prove by personal example that science is done by passionate human beings with prejudices, not by calculating machines or objective automatons."

HOBBIES AND OTHER INTERESTS

Gould is an avid reader who sprinkles his essays with references to such writers as Alexander Pope, George Eliot, William Shakespeare, George Orwell, and Michel de Montaigne. He enjoys music, particularly Bach and Gilbert and Sullivan, and he sings baritone with an amateur choral group, the Boston Cecilia Society. A devoted baseball fanatic, he is also a fan of the New York Yankees. Topics related to his favorite sport often creep into his essays, including one often-cited analysis of why there are no more .400 hitters in modern baseball. He discounts the usual explanations—that there are more night games, more travel, and fewer great hitters. Instead, he argues that all aspects of play have improved—hitting, pitching, and fielding. Because the skills of all baseball players have improved, there is a much smaller gap between the best hitters and the players they face on the field.

SELECTED WRITINGS

"Punctuated Equilibria: An Alternative to Phyletic Gradualism" (with Niles
    Eldredge), in *Models in Paleobiology*, edited by T.J.M. Schopf, 1972
Ontogeny and Phylogeny, 1977
Ever Since Darwin: Reflections in Natural History, 1977

The Panda's Thumb: More Reflections in Natural History, 1980
The Mismeasure of Man, 1981
Hen's Teeth and Horse's Toes: Further Reflections in Natural History, 1983
The Flamingo's Smile: Reflections in Natural History, 1985
An Urchin in the Storm: Essays about Books and Ideas, 1987
Time's Arrow, Time's Cycle: Myth and Metaphor in the Discovery of Geologic Time, 1987
Wonderful Life: The Burgess Shale and the Nature of History, 1989
Bully for Brontosaurus: Reflections in Natural History, 1991
Finders, Keepers, 1992
Eight Little Piggies: Reflections in Natural History, 1993
Dinosaur in a Haystack: Reflections in Natural History, 1995
Full House: The Spread of Excellence from Plato to Darwin, 1996
Questioning the Millennium: A Rationalist's Guide to a Precisely Arbitrary Countdown, 1997
Gould is also the editor and author of numerous technical scientific writings.

HONORS AND AWARDS

Schuchert Award (Paleontological Society): 1975, for excellence in research by a paleontologist under age 40
National Magazine Award for Essays and Criticism: 1980, for his column "This View of Life" in *Natural History* magazine
American Book Award for Science: 1981, for *The Panda's Thumb*
National Book Award for Science: 1981, for *The Panda's Thumb*
Scientist of the Year (*Discover* magazine): 1981, for his role in the Arkansas trial on teaching creationism in the public schools
National Book Critics Circle Award: 1981, for *The Mismeasure of Man*
John D. And Catherine T. MacArthur Foundation Prize Fellows Award: 1981
Medal of Excellence (Columbia University): 1982
Outstanding Book Award (American Educational Research Association): 1983, for *The Mismeasure of Man*
Bradford Washburn Award and Gold Medal (Museum of Science, Boston): 1984
Founders Council Award of Merit (Field Museum of Natural History, Chicago): 1984
Phi Beta Kappa Book Award in Science: 1984, for *Hen's Teeth and Horse's Toes*; 1990, for *Wonderful Life*
Distinguished Service Award (American Geological Institute): 1986
Harold D. Vursell Award (American Academy and Institute of Arts and Letters): 1987

Anthropology in Media Award (American Anthropological Association): 1987

History of Geology Award (Geological Society of America): 1988

Sue T. Friedman Medal (Geological Society of London): 1989

Britannica Award and Gold Medal: 1990

Forkosch Award: 1990, for *Wonderful Life*, for best book on a humanistic subject

Rhone-Poulenc Prize: 1991, for *Wonderful Life*

FURTHER READING

Books

Contemporary Authors New Revision Series, Vols. 27 and 56
Encyclopedia Britannica, 1995
International Who's Who, 1996-97
Thinkers of the Twentieth Century, 2nd. ed., 1987
Who's Who in America, 1997

Periodicals

AB Bookman's Weekly, June 25, 1990, p.2713
Boston Magazine, Jan. 1996, p.127
Current Biography Yearbook 1982
Esquire, Jan. 1997, p.112
Mother Jones, Jan.-Feb. 1997, p.60
New York Times, Feb. 11, 1993, p.C1
New York Times Biographical Service, Nov. 1983, p.1331; Feb. 1993, p.220
New York Times Magazine, Nov. 20, 1983, p.48
Newsweek, Mar. 29, 1982, p.44; Nov. 20, 1989, p.68
People, Dec. 8, 1980, p.151; June 2, 1986, p.109
Publishers Weekly, Oct. 13, 1989, p.32
Rolling Stone, Jan. 15, 1987, p.38
Time, May 14, 1990, p.19

ADDRESS

Harvard University
Museum of Comparative Zoology
Department of Earth Sciences
Cambridge, MA 02138

Shirley Ann Jackson 1946-
American Physicist
Chairman of the U.S. Nuclear Regulatory
Commission
First African-American Woman in the U.S. to Earn a
Ph.D. in Physics

BIRTH

Shirley Ann Jackson was born in Washington, D.C., on August
5, 1946. Her mother, Beatrice (Cosby) Jackson, was a social
worker, and her father, George Jackson, worked for the post of
fice. The Jacksons lived in the predominantly black northwest
district of Washington, where Shirley and her sister, Gloria, re-

ceived a great deal of support and encouragement from the community around them.

YOUTH

Education was very important to the Jackson family. Shirley's mother helped her daughter develop good reading and writing skills. She would read stories to her daughter about famous African-Americans like the mathematician and astronomer Benjamin Banneker, the poet Paul Laurence Dunbar, and the educator Mary McLeod Bethune. Shirley's father, who had always been interested in math and science, helped her with her science projects. "I was very interested in nutrition," she recalls. "[My father] helped me with my experiments growing molds and bacteria in our kitchen." She was a curious child who enjoyed figuring out how things worked, especially the go-carts she built out of soap boxes with her sister Gloria.

But Jackson's natural curiosity might have never blossomed without her parents' help. "I give most of the credit to my parents for helping me identify my natural inclinations and abilities at an early age," she now says. "I had always been a curious child, anxious to know how things worked. This natural curiosity, though, would never have carried me very far without the skills and values that my parents passed on to me. . . . [Both] of them encouraged me to study hard and excel. They were my ultimate role models in the way they lived their lives and dealt with adversity."

Shirley's talent for science was evident at an early age, and her friends routinely called her "The Brain." She once told her mother that some day she would be called, "Shirley the Great," but she could not foresee the barriers that would stand in her way as an African-American woman in a male-dominated field.

EARLY MEMORIES

As a young girl, Shirley was very interested in biology and often collected live insects so she could observe their behavior in different environments. One experiment that she remembers vividly involved collecting live bumblebees and feeding them sugar to see how diet affected their lives. She kept the bees in glass jars, which she stored underneath the back porch in a crawl space. "You would come out on the porch and hear all the buzzing from 20 or 30 jars," she recalls.

EDUCATION

Jackson loved school while she was growing up. "School was my thing," she says. "It was the focus of my young life." She enjoyed everything—reading, science, and math—but as she explains here, "I especially liked and did well in mathematics. I liked to play and make up games with numbers for people to solve. One of my science projects was building a slide rule based on a binary system."

Most schools in Washington, D.C., were segregated when Jackson was growing up. White children went to one school and black children went to another. Even though the Jackson family lived just three blocks from an excellent school in a predominantly white neighborhood, she and her sister were driven miles across town so they could attend a black elementary school. But she still feels that her educational experience in Washington was a good one. In 1954, the U.S. Supreme Court outlawed segregated schools for blacks and whites. Jackson attended an integrated middle school, but her high school was predominately African-American.

―――― " ――――

"I give most of the credit to my parents for helping me identify my natural inclinations and abilities at an early ages. I had always been a curious child, anxious to know how things worked. This natural curiosity, though, would never have carried me very far without the skills and values that my parents passed on to me. . . . [Both] of them encouraged me to study hard and excel. They were my ultimate role models in the way they lived their lives and dealt with adversity."

―――― " ――――

When the Russians sent the first satellite, known as Sputnik, into space in 1957, the United States decided it was time to develop more scientific talent among its young people. Jackson entered an accelerated science and math program at Roosevelt High School. This program enabled her to complete all her required courses by the end of her junior year, leaving her free to spend senior year taking advanced subjects. During high school Jackson also participated in a club called "Teens of Personality," a group that she and other girls formed for studying, socializing, and academic support. "We all liked and excelled in different subjects—English, biology, history," she recalls. "I was the math whiz and had an interest in science. But I had a lot of interests—reading the classics in Latin, poetry, history, especially the history or the great wars of the world. Given my interests, you wouldn't have necessarily predicted that I'd become a scientist." She was a straight-A student who looked to her teachers—most of them black women—as role models. She graduated from Roosevelt High as valedictorian of her class in 1964.

Attending College at MIT

Jackson was given a scholarship to attend the Massachusetts Institute of Technology (MIT) in Boston. But no one at the college really expected her to do well. No student from a black public high school had ever been admitted to MIT before, and when she used the elevator, she was often mistaken for the elevator operator. People didn't understand why a black woman would be interested in physics. One professor told her that she shouldn't major in physics "because colored girls should learn a trade." Most of her professors just ignored her. There was one administrator who would meet with her each semester because of her scholarship. As she recalls here, "At the end of the year he said, 'Well, gee Miss Jackson, we thought we were throwing a kitten in among the tigers. But you turned out to be a tiger!"

Jackson was one of only five African-Americans — only two of whom were female — in her freshman class of 900. Yet she was unprepared for how lonely she would feel at MIT. The white women students refused to share her table in the cafeteria, and they made it clear that they didn't want to include her in their study groups. "I went through a down period," she admits, "but at some level you have to decide you will persist in what you're doing and that you won't let people beat you down."

Despite this treatment, Jackson loved her classes. During her freshman year she developed an interest in physics, which she described as "a good marriage of mathematics and the natural world." One of her first assignments in her introductory physics class was to estimate the number of blades of grass in the MIT courtyard — an exercise designed to teach students how to do quick calculations and to understand physical laws and the principles of symmetry. Jackson persevered with her studies, despite her feelings of isolation and loneliness. She gradually earned the grudging respect of her professors and the other students as she proved, beyond question, her ability to do the work. Jackson earned her bachelor's degree from MIT in 1968.

Graduate Studies

When she graduated, Jackson was offered a fellowship to continue her studies and get her Ph.D. (or doctorate) at MIT. She was also accepted at Brown, Harvard, and the University of Chicago for graduate school, but she decided to remain at MIT so that she could encourage more African-American students to apply there. Along with other African-American MIT students, she organized the Black Student Union (BSU). They prodded the university to admit more black students. Ultimately, MIT began identifying eligible minority students and recruiting them for the university. MIT also created a more flexible admissions policy, a financial aid plan, and an orientation program for incoming minority students. Dr. Paul Gray, the former president of MIT, had

Shirley Jackson and her Japanese counterpart Yasumasa Togo shake hands after signing a nuclear safety agreement in 1997.

this to say about Jackson's role in that process. "Shirley Jackson was the most significant and important constructive force in our group. . . . [She] stands out in my mind as being one of the best bridge builders during that difficult time. Her manner was always calm, unassuming, and reassuring. All of us — administrators, faculty, and students — are in Shirley's debt for her help in opening MIT up to equal opportunity for black and other non-white students."

For her doctoral work at MIT, Jackson studied theoretical elementary particle physics. This is the branch of physics that uses theories and mathematics to predict the existence of subatomic particles — the tiny units of which all matter is made — and the forces that bind them together. Here is Jackson's description of her work: "I worked in what was then known as interacting physics, where one uses mathematics to study the forces holding protons and neutrons together in the nucleus of an atom."

Jackson received her Ph.D. in theoretical elementary particle physics in 1973. She was the first black woman to earn a doctorate from MIT and the first black woman in the country to receive a Ph.D. in physics. But she had done more than make academic history. During her years at MIT, she served as co-chair and then adviser to the Black Student Union. She also tutored young people at the YMCA in Boston's predominantly black Roxbury section. In other words, she did everything she could to encourage other young black students to follow in her footsteps.

After leaving MIT, Jackson spent the years 1973 to 1976 doing postgraduate work. She studied at the Fermi National Accelerator Laboratory in Batavia, Illinois, which was named for Enrico Fermi, a physicist who produced the first self-sustaining nuclear chain reaction. She also did postgraduate work at the European Center for Nuclear Research (CERN) in Geneva, Switzerland. In addition, she traveled to several European countries to lecture and present scientific papers on her research. Jackson enjoyed the experience of living in Europe. "It was a lot easier than living in the United States. There were a lot of tensions here racially, and I was away from this in Switzerland, free to concentrate on my science. I was the only black at CERN, but everybody was international. It was very stimulating, both intellectually and personally."

—— *"* ——

"I model the semiconductor system mathematically. That is, I use math to explain to other scientists what's going on in the things they've observed in the laboratory experiments. If I build a math model, I can predict what will happen when the temperature of the conductor is lowered or what wavelength of light will be transmitted at different temperatures."

—— *"* ——

CAREER HIGHLIGHTS

AT&T Bell Labs

In 1976 Jackson joined the staff as a theoretical physicist at AT&T Bell Laboratories in Murray Hill, New Jersey. The AT&T Bell Labs are considered among the world's finest industrial research facilities for their pioneering research into information technology and telecommunications. In 1978 she joined the Scattering and Low Energy Physics Research Department at AT&T Bell Labs. Ten years later, in 1988, she moved to the Solid State and Quantum Physics Research Department. Her research included the areas of theoretical physics, solid state and quantum physic, and optical physics.

At Bell Labs, Jackson's research focused on examining the properties of various materials in an effort to find better ways of using them for voice and data communications. To that end, she studied the electronic and optical properties of certain materials to understand how effectively they can transmit, store, and use electricity. She used advanced mathematical problems to describe matter in motion. For example, in her work on semiconductors, Jackson would develop a series of questions about the properties of the semiconductors and then create mathematical word problems to correspond to those questions. These calculations could predict what would happen under certain laboratory conditions. As Jackson herself once explained it, "I model the semiconductor system mathematically. That is, I use math to explain to other scientists what's going on in the things they've observed in the laboratory experiments. If I build a math model, I can predict what will happen when the temperature of the conductor is lowered or what wavelength of light will be transmitted at different temperatures." The ground breaking work that Jackson performed in her 15 years at AT&T Bell Labs made a significant contribution to the field of communications and won her the recognition of scientists all over the world.

Teacher and MIT Board Member

In 1985, while still working at Bell Labs, Jackson entered the world of public affairs when governor Thomas Kean appointed her to the New Jersey Commission on Science and Technology. She has also served on committees for the National Academy of Sciences, the American Association for the Advancement of Science, and the National Science Foundation. In each of these positions, she has made her mark by promoting not just science, but the advancement of women and African-Americans in her field. One of the greatest honors Jackson has received is her appointment as a life member of the Board of Trustees at MIT — the same institution where she had once been a lonely female minority student.

In 1991, Jackson left AT&T Bell Labs and re-entered the academic world as a professor of physics at Rutgers University in New Jersey. "I wanted to have graduate students," she explains, "and to build my own research groups." She taught at Rutgers for four years, although she maintained her connection to AT&T Bell Labs during this time by serving as a consultant in semiconductor theory.

Chairman of the NRC

In February 1995, President Bill Clinton nominated Shirley Ann Jackson to the Nuclear Regulatory Commission (NRC). After being confirmed by the U.S. Senate, she was sworn in on May 2, 1995, She assumed the chairmanship of the NRC two months later, on July 1, 1995. The Commission has five members, one of whom is designated chairman by the President. Jackson is both the first woman and the first African-American to serve in this position.

The NRC is a federal agency whose job is to guarantee the safety of all the nuclear power plants in the U.S. The NRC sets standards and rules pertaining to nuclear facilities, issues licenses, and conducts inspections and investigations. Its responsibilities include protecting public health and safety, protecting the environment, and protecting and safeguarding materials and nuclear facilities. Overall, the NRC is charged with safeguarding the public from the health and safety hazards associated with nuclear power. As Chairman, Jackson is the principal executive officer and official spokesperson of the NRC. She is responsible for overseeing all functions relating to administration, long-range planning, budgeting, and personnel issues.

When she accepted the chairmanship of the NRC, Shirley Ann Jackson took on not only a federal agency with 3,000 employees but the challenge of dealing with an industry whose future is at best uncertain. The dangers associated with nuclear energy became impossible to ignore with the near-meltdown at the Three Mile Island nuclear plant in 1979 and the Chernobyl nuclear power disaster in Russia in 1986. In the U.S., most of the 110 nuclear power plants are aging, and the problem of storing nuclear waste remains largely unsolved. A number of plants have been under attack from "whistle blowers." These are usually nuclear plant employees who believe that their employers are not obeying established safety rules and who take their complaints directly to the NRC.

Shortly after Jackson took charge of the NRC, a huge controversy erupted over nuclear power. Two engineers at the Millstone I power plant in Waterford, Connecticut, "blew the whistle" on their employer after complaining for two years that radioactive fuel rods were being moved into a storage pool that was already crowded with thousands of old fuel rods. An investigation revealed that the NRC knew about the safety violation but had allowed the plant to continue operating anyway. In March 1996 *Time* magazine featured a cover story on nuclear safety, drawing attention to the federal government's failure to enforce its own rules.

Jackson responded to the crisis by ordering a nationwide review of all 110 nuclear power plants to see how many of them had been moving fuel rods in violation of the Commission's safety standards. She shut down all three Millstone plants and took steps to improve the skills of NRC inspectors and staff members. Although the NRC is still dealing with many of the problems revealed by the nationwide review, Jackson's handling of the situation won her the admiration of those on both sides of the controversy. In May 1997, she was elected chair of the International Nuclear Regulator's Association, a new group that was formed by the regulatory officials of Canada, France, Germany, Japan, Spain, the United Kingdom, and the U.S.

MARRIAGE AND FAMILY

Jackson met her future husband, Dr. Morris A. Washington, while she was working at AT&T Bell Labs. Although he is also a physicist who works for Lucent Technologies, Dr. Washington is occasionally addressed as "Mr. Jackson." He doesn't seem to mind the publicity that his wife's career has brought her, nor does Jackson mind being called "Mrs. Washington" on occasion. Both seem quite willing to play the role of supportive spouse when circumstances call for it.

Jackson's job as head of the NRC means that she must spend all week in Washington, D.C. On weekends she returns to New Jersey to spend time with her husband and their son, Alan, who was born in 1981. Shirley's sister, Gloria, is an attorney who also lives in Washington.

HOBBIES AND OTHER INTERESTS

Jackson has never shied away from trying new activities. She took up photography in her 20s because she didn't like "other people's representations of life." In her 40s, she decided that since she had always wanted to play the piano, she might as well begin taking lessons. Over the years she has also been an avid tennis player, hiker, and bicyclist.

HONORS AND AWARDS

Karl Taylor Compton Award (Massachusetts Institute of Technology): 1970, for outstanding contributions as an undergraduate
Outstanding Young Women of America Award: 1976, 1981
Salute to Policy Makers Award (Executive Women of New Jersey): 1986
Black Achievers in Industry Award (Harlem YMCA): 1986
New Jersey Governor's Award: 1993

FURTHER READING

Books

African Americans: Voices of Triumph, 1993
Contemporary Black Biography, 1996, Vol. 12
Hayden, Robert C. *Seven African American Scientists,* 1992
Notable Black American Women, 1992
Notable Twentieth-Century Scientists, 1995
Who's Who among African-Americans, 1996
Who's Who in America, 1997

Periodicals

Black Enterprise, Feb. 1985, p.49
Christian Science Monitor, Nov. 20, 1989, People section, p.14
Ebony, Nov. 1974, p.114; July 1996, p.115

Science, Apr. 16, 1993, p.393
Time, Mar. 4, 1996, p.46; Mar. 17, 1997, p.34
Washington Post, May 4, 1995, p.B10

ADDRESS

U.S. Nuclear Regulatory Commission
Washington, D.C. 20555

Raymond Kurzweil 1948-

American Inventor and Entrepreneur
Inventor of the Kurzweil Reading Machine, Kurzweil
250 Electronic Synthesizer, and Kurzweil VoiceWriter

BIRTH

Raymond Kurzweil was born February 12, 1948, in New York
City, New York. His mother, Hannah Kurzweil, was a successful
artist and illustrator, and his father, Fredric Kurzweil, was a well-
known concert pianist and conductor with the Bell Symphony
Orchestra who began teaching young Raymond to play piano
when he was just six. His parents raised Raymond and his sister
Enid in Queens, New York, where they emphasized the arts and

education. As his sister recalls, "The religion in our family wasn't Jewish, it was intellectualism."

YOUTH

"I remember very distinctly, ever since I was five, knowing that I'd be a scientist, and knowing that I'd be a famous one, a very successful one," Kurzweil once said. "I even kept a notebook of inventions when I was five, six, and seven years old. I still have it. The idea of inventing and being a scientist was all wrapped up together for me. At the time, I was very interested in building things—with my Erector set, for example—and I also remember trying to build a rocket."

This childhood confidence was due at least in part to Kurzweil's extended family. His relatives, who had established themselves in a wide range of professions, encouraged him to make good use of his gifts. In addition to his mother and father, who were highly regarded in the fields of art and music, respectively, Kurzweil had several other family members that he could look to as career models. His grandfather was a doctor, a couple of his uncles were engineers, and one was a successful inventor. "But when I really think about it," said Kurzweil, "the relative who might have had the most influence on me as a scientist was my grandmother Lillian Bader. She was somewhat of a famous scientist and the first woman in Europe to get a Ph.D. in chemistry. She traveled around Europe lecturing and also ran a major school that her mother had started, so she was actually both a scientist and an entrepreneur."

By the time Kurzweil was 12 years old, his natural intelligence and curiosity led him to computers, which were still rare at that time. Before long he was devoting hours of his spare time to various computer programs and projects, and his entire family noticed that he seemed to have a great aptitude for the machines. In 1961 one of his uncles got him a summer job at the Institute for Developmental Studies in New York, where he quickly made his mark by writing a computer program that featured very advanced statistical methods. This program showed so much promise that International Business Machines (IBM), the largest computer company in the world, bought the program from him and made it available to scientists around the country. Kurzweil was just 13 a the time. "He always thought on a much larger scale than everyone else," recalled his sister Enid. "He would never put up a little tent in the backyard. He always had to turn the entire house and lawn into a fortress."

This habit of thinking big continued to serve Kurzweil well during his teenage years, and he soon became adept at building his own computers. At the age of 16 he developed a computer program that combined his background in music with his interest it computers. Kurzweil's program analyzed the style of musical compositions and composed music in a way that approximated the output of some of the world's greatest composers. "If you fed it Mozart, it would generate original melodies that sounded pleasant but which didn't have the genius of Mozart," Kurzweil recalled. "The music sounded like it came from one of his second-rate students." At the time, though, Kurzweil's program caused a tremendous sensation. That project, along with his creation of a computer software program that could guide a mouse through a maze, won him a coveted Westinghouse Science Talent Search Award and established Kurzweil as one of America's most talented young computer geniuses.

> "
>
> *"I remember very distinctly, ever since I was five, knowing that I'd be a scientist, and knowing that I'd be a famous one, a very successful one. I even kept a notebook of inventions when I was five, six, and seven years old. I still have it. The idea of inventing and being a scientist was all wrapped up together for me. At the time, I was very interested in building things — with my Erector set, for example — and I also remember trying to build a rocket."*
>
> "

EDUCATION

Kurzweil graduated from Martin Van Buren High School in New York City in 1965. Later that fall he began his college course work at the prestigious Massachusetts Institute of Technology (MIT), where he distinguished himself even among his elite classmates as a particularly bright and ambitious young man. He posted top grades throughout his time at MIT, even though he rarely attended classes or other normal college activities. Instead, he spent most of his time writing poetry or working on his own computer projects. These characteristics soon led his classmates to call him "The Phantom."

"MIT was very oriented towards students who took initiative," Kurzweil recalled. "For example, I took off one whole semester to get a company I had started off the ground and received course credit for it. The company was built around [a software program] I had developed for matching high school students with colleges. It had several million facts on 3,000 colleges in the United States in its memory and a 300-question questionnaire for students to fill out. Based on their answers, the expert system would give them a list of 15 colleges that they might want to look into. I sold that system [for $100,000] to Harcourt Brace World, which is now Harcourt Brace Jovanovich."

Raymond Kurzweil and the Kurzweil Reading Machine

Yet despite his obvious talent on computers and that big $100,000 pay-check—half of which he gave to his parents—Kurzweil was undecided during college about how he wanted to spend his adult life. The young computer genius had also developed into a talented poet, and his love for literature continued to grow under the tutelage of playwright Lillian Hellman and other university professors. "He really seriously considered trying to become a poet and forgetting about his scientific abilities," recalled one of Kurzweil's college roommates. As time passed, however, it became obvious to him that he would probably be much more financially successful as a computer programmer than as a poet, and he decided to make poetry a beloved hobby instead of a profession. Kurzweil graduated from MIT in 1970. He earned a B.S. (bachelor of science degree) with a double major in literature and computer science.

CAREER HIGHLIGHTS

After graduating from MIT, Kurzweil spent four years working as a consultant to computer software firms. In his spare time, meanwhile, he worked on developing a computer that could ready any style of typeface. This problem had baffled programmers for years. Although a few computer models had shown an ability to "read" a few specific typefaces, no one had been able to figure out how to put together a program with "omni font character capacity" — the ability to recognize any type font regardless of its style. "It was a fascinating problem," said Kurzweil. "It wasn't something that I developed in a flash in the shower or in two showers. It was a painstaking effort of trail and error."

In 1974 Kurzweil launched a company called Kurzweil Computer Products to find a solution to this puzzle. He borrowed $200,000 from friends and family to establish the company, which he based in the Boston area, and he hired several talented engineers to help him. But as the months passed and a solution proved elusive, he noticed that he was rapidly running out of money. About 18 months after the company had been founded, Kurzweil found it very difficult to pay even small bills, and the telephone company told him that they would cut off his service if he did not pay them what he owed. Despondent, Kurzweil took some lab equipment to a pawn shop to sell. But when he walked in the door, a dog owned by another customer bit him in the leg. The dog owner promptly offered Kurzweil $50 in compensation for the injury and the programmer happily took it. The unexpected windfall allowed him to pay off the phone company without selling any of his laboratory equipment, and seemed to signal a change in the business's fortunes. A few months later, Kurzweil and his fellow engineers finally unveiled the Kurzweil Reading Machine.

Kurzweil Reading Machine

The Kurzweil Reading Machine (KRM) was presented to the world on January 13, 1976, and the product and its principal creator were immediately showered with praise. Not only had Kurzweil attacked the problem of typeface recognition, he had also put that knowledge to practical use by making a product that scanned printed materials and converted it into spoken words. All users had to do was place the article or book on top of the reading machine, and the device would read the information aloud. Armed with such a machine, blind people could enjoy a wide range of printed material, including books and newspapers that had long been off-limits to them. Observers marveled at the inventor's talent and ingenuity, and many people stated that the KRM was the most important development for blind people since the introduction of the Braille alphabet.

In the days and weeks following the unveiling of the Kurzweil Reading Machine, Kurzweil made appearances on all three major television networks, and his invention was prominently featured in major newspapers around the country. Shortly after making an appearance on "The Today Show," the inventor received a telephone call from Stevie Wonder, the famous blind musician. Kurzweil recalled that Wonder was "very excited about it and wanted [a machine] right away, so we actually turned the factory upside down and produced a unit that day. We showed him how to hook it up himself. He left with it practically under his arm. I understand he took it straight to his hotel room, set it up, and read all night." Wonder himself agreed that the machine became a source of great joy to him, calling it "a brother and a friend . . . without question, another sunshine of my life." Indeed, in the years immediately after its invention, the KRM became an essential piece of equipment for libraries and other institutions that provide services to blind people. In 1978 Kurzweil introduced the Kurzweil Data Entry Machine (KDEM), a version of the KRM that was specifically created for commercial data entry purposes.

Launching New Companies

The tremendous success of the Kurzweil Reading Machine made Kurzweil eager to take on other challenges, and by the end of 1979 he decided to expand the company's operations. "We decided the best way to do that was to sell the company to Xerox," Kurzweil stated. "In 1980, Kurzweil Computer Products was sold to Xerox, with the understanding that it would remain an independent company with the same management that I had originally put in place. I stayed on as full-time president and CEO. In mid-1982, I worked out an arrangement with Xerox to start two other companies—Kurzweil Music and Kurzweil Applied Intelligence—while still retaining my position as chairman at Kurzweil Computer Products." Xerox paid him approximately $6 million for the company, which gave him plenty of funding to start his new enterprises.

Years later, Kurzweil recalled that it was a casual conversation with Stevie Wonder, who had become a friend of his over the years, that had inspired him to launch Kurzweil Music Systems (KMS). "I was visiting Stevie in California [in 1982] and he was showing me his studio and various electronic instruments and was lamenting the fact that there were really two different worlds of music"—the acoustic world of traditional instruments and the electronic world of synthesized music. "He said, 'Wouldn't it be great if we could use these very powerful artistic control methods that electronics provides to control the rich, beautiful sounds of the acoustic world?'" Intrigued by Wonder's thoughts, Kurzweil decided to try to make a synthesizer that would be able to accurately reproduce the sounds of guitars, violins, pianos, flutes, saxophones, and other instruments. Within two years of establishing Kurzweil Music Systems, Kurzweil had created the Kurzweil 250 synthesizer by utilizing artificial intelligence, pattern recognition technology, and signal processing advances. This synthesizer, recalled the inventor, "was widely recognized as the first electronic instrument that really sounded like a piano, or a violin, or whatever orchestral instrument you were trying to emulate. It very quickly became the dominant instrument in its price range, which was $10,000 to $20,000, and became standard in studios for doing movie and television scores."

Meanwhile, Kurzweil's other company, Kurzweil Applied Intelligence, was making strides of its own. By the mid-1980s the company, which was housed in the same Boston-area building as Kurzweil Music Systems, was producing voice-activated word processing machines that typed words on a screen as they were spoken by the user. Early versions of the machine only recognized a few hundred spoken words, but by 1987 Kurzweil and his engineers had created a system that used 10,000 words. This device, known as the Kurzweil VoiceWriter, became particularly popular in the medical market, as doctors and nurses learned that they could generate printed medical reports simply by speaking into the computer. Since then, other applications have been developed that aid the disabled. For example, the machine has been used by paraplegics, those who have lost the use of their arms and legs, to control robot arms that perform services for them. The voice recognition system has also been used in children's hospitals for kids who cannot manipulate a keyboard. And research has been done to see if it could translate the impaired speech of those with cerebral palsy.

> "
>
> *"If I were to define what I do, I would say that I help develop technology to solve some previously unsolved human problems. That's where the excitement comes in — to have a blind person go to school because the technology can help him or her read or to have a musician create a new piece of music that wasn't feasible before."*
>
> "

During the same year, when Kurzweil was creating the Kurzweil VoiceWriter, he was also featured in a documentary called *The Age of Intelligent Machines*.

His already significant reputation as a visionary computer wizard was greatly increased by the documentary and the voice recognition system. "The science behind the technology I'm working on today still fascinates me," he said. "If I were to define what I do, I would say that I help develop technology to solve some previously unsolved human problems. That's where the excitement comes in — to have a blind person go to school because the technology can help him or her read or to have a musician create a new piece of music that wasn't feasible before."

Financial Troubles

But even as Kurzweil's reputation as a talented inventor grew, observers speculated that he was less skilled as a businessman. Everybody agreed that his inventions were incredible, but many analysts claimed that his companies overestimated the number of sales that they would be able to make on their products. Others pointed out that research costs in Kurzweil's companies tended to be very high, and that he increasingly had to borrow large amounts of money to keep the businesses afloat. Also, financial analysts noted that it often takes advanced technology companies several years to become profitable. "I consider myself a) an inventor and b) an entrepreneur," Kurzweil says. "Each of these tends to develop skills and get better with experience. It's a matter of combining your knowledge of the world with learning how to put people together and systems together."

> **"I consider myself a) an inventor and b) an entrepreneur. Each of these tends to develop skills and get better with experience. It's a matter of combining your knowledge of the world with learning how to put people together and systems together."**

Despite Kurzweil's best efforts, KMS continued to perform poorly because of increased competition and the perception that its products were overpriced. Early in 1990, shortly after KMS filed for bankruptcy protection, a piano manufacturer called Young Chang America purchased the company. Kurzweil stayed on as a technical consultant, but the purchase freed him to spend a lot more time attending to the needs of Kurzweil Applied Intelligence.

In the early 1990s, it appeared that Kurzweil Applied Intelligence was gaining strength financially. Kurzweil's brilliance was still seen as a big company asset, and a 1993 public stock offering (in which ownership shares in the company are made available for investors to buy) proved successful.

Encouraged by the apparent upturn in the company's fortunes, Kurzweil turned his attention to writing. But instead of writing a book about inventions or entrepreneurship, he wrote about his growing interest in the relationship between diet and overall physical health. In 1993 his book *The 10-Percent Solution for a Healthy Life: How to Eliminate Virtually All Risk of Heart Disease and Cancer* was published. In its pages he explained that both his father and grandfather had died of heart disease at relatively young ages. These losses had spurred him to do a lot of research on diet and physical health, and he eventually came to the conclusion that too many Americans relied on diets that were too high in fat and calories. Kurzweil argued that dietary recommendations from the American Heart Association and other groups were too mild, and that people should limit fat consumption to one-tenth of a day's calories and restrict their intake of salt, cholesterol, nicotine, and alcohol. He contended that if people combined these dietary guidelines with regular aerobic exercise and stress management, they would be far less likely to fall victim to heart disease, cancer, and other illnesses. Some people were amazed that Kurzweil was able to find the time to write a diet book while simultaneously attending to the needs of his company, but those who knew him well were not surprised. "He's 110 percent into everything he does, whether it's from his diet to his inventions," said one business associate.

Company Rocked by Scandal

Kurzweil's happiness about the publication of his book proved short-lived, however. In April 1994 authorities charged that several executives with Kurzweil Applied Intelligence had engaged in deceitful business activities over the previous 18 months. Investigators revealed that the company's president, its vice president of sales, and two other officers had misled investors during the company's 1993 stock sale by recording sales for potential customers who had not yet signed final sales agreements. In fact, they had booked millions of dollars in phony sales. These actions made the company seem healthier than it actually was, which led many investors to buy stock in the company at a price that was higher than its actual value.

Kurzweil did not know about the scheme, and he fired the executives as soon as he learned about it. But the damage was done. In 1996, the dishonest officers were found guilty and sentenced to jail terms for conspiracy, securities fraud, and falsifying company records. By then, the value of the tarnished company's stock had plummeted. Many analysts wondered whether the business would be able to survive. In April 1997, though, Kurzweil Applied Intelligence agreed to be acquired for about $53 million by Lernout & Hauspie Speech Products N.V., a voice recognition company based in Belgium. The company announced that Kurzweil would stay on as a consultant to the combined company.

MARRIAGE AND FAMILY

Kurzweil married Sonya Rosenwald, a psychologist, on August 3, 1975. They live with their two children, Ethan and Amy, in the suburban Boston area.

HOBBIES AND OTHER INTERESTS

Despite his ambitious work schedule, Kurzweil still finds time to enjoy several hobbies. He continues to read and write poetry whenever he can, and he is an accomplished pianist. Kurzweil also has been heavily involved in a variety of philanthropic and educational areas over the years. He has served as a trustee of Boston's Beth Israel Hospital, an overseer of the New England Conservatory of Music, a founder of Boston's Museum of Science, and a director of the Boston Computer Society.

WRITINGS

The Age of Intelligent Machines, 1990
The 10-Percent Solution for a Healthy Life: How to Eliminate Virtually All Risk of Heart Disease and Cancer, 1993

HONORS AND AWARDS

First Prize in Electronics and Communications (International Science Fair): 1965
Massachusetts Governor's Award: 1977
Grace Murray Hopper Outstanding Young Computer Scientist of Year Award (Association for Computing Machinery): 1978
Personal Computing to Aid the Handicapped National Award (Johns Hopkins University): 1981
Computer Industry Hall of Fame: 1982
Francis Joseph Campbell Award (American Library Association): 1983
Best of the New Generation Award (*Esquire* magazine): 1984
Distinguished Inventor Award (Intellectual Property Owners): 1986
White House Award for Entrepreneurial Excellence: 1986
Honorary Chairman for Innovation (White House Conference on Small Business): 1986
Chris Plaque (Columbus International Film Festival): 1987, for documentary *The Age of Intelligent Machines*
Gold Medal for Science Education (International Film and TV Festival of New York): 1987, for documentary *The Age of Intelligent Machines*
CINE Golden Eagle: 1987, for documentary *The Age of Intelligent Machines*
New England Inventor of the Year: 1988
Founders Award (Massachusetts Institute of Technology): 1989

Engineer of the Year Award (*Design News* magazine): 1990
Most Outstanding Computer Science Book of 1990 (Association of
  American Publishers): 1991, for book *The Age of Intelligent Machines*
Louis Braille Award (Associated Services for the Blind): 1991

FURTHER READING

Books

Aronoff, Craig E., and John L. Ward, eds. *Contemporary Entrepreneurs,* 1992
Brown, Kenneth A. *Inventors at Work,* 1988
Contemporary Authors, Vol. 134
Gilder, George. *Microcosm: The Quantum Revolution in Economics and
  Technology,* 1989
Notable Twentieth-Century Scientists, 1995
Who's Who in America, 1990-91
The Writer's Directory, 1996-98

Periodicals

Audio, Jan. 1989, p.62
Boston Globe, July 26, 1983; July 27, 1995, p.35; Dec. 13, 1996, p.C16; Apr. 16,
  1997, p.C2
Compass Readings, Apr. 1990, p.24
Computers & Electronics, July 1984, p.40
Computerworld, Mar. 18, 1991, p.75
Connoisseur, Apr. 1984, p.118
Esquire, Dec. 1984, p.118
New York, Apr. 8, 1985, p.19
Omni, Feb. 1985, p.86
People, Feb. 9, 1976, p.55; Mar. 9, 1987, p.113
Popular Mechanics, Oct. 1987, p.69
Reader's Digest, Feb. 1991, p.119
Science Digest, Feb. 1984, p.73
Sciquest, Feb. 1981, p.21
Time, Apr. 28, 1986, p.54
U.S. News & World Report, June 13, 1983, p.61
Wall Street Journal, May 24, 1994, p.B7

ADDRESS

Kurzweil Applied Intelligence, Inc.
411 Waverly Oaks Rd.
Waltham, MA 02154

Shannon Lucid 1943-

American Biochemist and Astronaut
Holds American Record for Longest Time in Space

BIRTH

Shannon Lucid was born Shannon Wells in Shanghai, China, on
January 14, 1943. Her parents, Joseph and Myrtle Wells, were
Baptist missionaries from the United States who were living in
China at the time of Shannon's birth. She is the oldest of four
children, with one sister, Anne, and two brothers, John and Joe.

GROWING UP

Shannon's early years were marked by danger and deprivation.

She was born during World War II in China, which was an ally of the U.S. against Japan in that war. When she was just six weeks old, Shannon and her parents were captured by Japanese soldiers and put in a prisoner of war camp. The family nearly starved. Her parents saved their meager, moldy rice rations to feed their infant daughter. "My wife would skim the worms off the top and mix up powdered milk with it," Joseph Wells remembered. Somehow, they survived. After a year in the camp, they were released in a prisoner exchange and moved back to the U.S.

After the war was over, the Wells family returned to China, where the parents resumed their missionary work. In 1949, when Mao Zedong and the communists took over the country, the Wells and all other missionaries were forced to leave. They settled in Bethany, Oklahoma. Joseph Wells worked as an evangelist preacher, speaking at religious revivals all over the country.

YOUTH

As a young child, Shannon loved tales of the early pioneers, and she wanted to be a pioneer, too. She was a bit discouraged when she found out that most of the world had already been explored, but then she discovered space. She decided she would be a space pioneer. "Well, shoot, I can be a space explorer," she remembers thinking. "Nobody's going to get all space explored before I grow up. . . . People thought I was crazy because that was long before America had a space program."

EDUCATION

Shannon attended the public schools in Bethany and always did well. She especially loved math and science. When she was in junior high, she found a book on Robert Goddard, an American physicist and rocket expert. She wrote a paper on Goddard and his achievements, in which she stated that she, too, wanted to be a rocket scientist. Her teacher discouraged her, saying that "even if there was a job like that, she wouldn't be able to have it, because she was a girl." But Shannon wasn't about to be put off by such antiquated, sexist ways of thinking. She kept her dream alive.

When she was in eighth grade, Shannon started experimenting with chemicals to try to make fuel for her own rocket. When she went to the local drug store to buy the chemicals she needed, the pharmacist wouldn't sell them to her he thought she would blow something up. He called her science teacher, who assured him that Shannon was indeed working on a science assignment. Shannon got her chemicals and did her experiment.

In high school, Shannon found a wonderful science teacher, Blanche Moon, who encouraged her dreams of becoming a scientist. Later, when she became an astronaut, Lucid got back in touch with Moon and has invited her to each of her NASA launchings.

Lucid also followed another ambition, to become a pilot. She took flying classes after high school and earned her pilot's license. She would sometimes fly her father to his preaching engagements in an old Piper Clipper she had bought. Her dad remembers her saying that "the Baptists wouldn't let women preach, so I had to become an astronaut to get closer to God than my father." Later, after she had logged thousands of miles, she tried to get training as a commercial pilot, but she was turned down because she was a woman. "I used to tell myself that I only wanted a job because I was qualified, not because I was a woman," Lucid remembered. "Then, after a while, I began to wonder whether it might not be nice to be somebody's token woman."

After graduating second in her class at Bethany High School in 1960, Lucid went on to the University of Oklahoma, where she was the first woman to major in chemistry. She received her bachelor of science degree in chemistry in just three years, graduating in 1963.

Combining Work and School

After graduating from college in 1963, Lucid took a series of jobs in her field. From 1963 to 1964, she served as a teaching assistant at the University of Oklahoma's Department of Chemistry. In 1964, she took a job as a senior lab technician at the Oklahoma Medical Research Foundation, where she worked for two years. She worked for a chemical company from 1966 to 1968, where she met her husband, Michael Lucid.

Returning to the University of Oklahoma in 1969, Lucid worked for the Health Science Center's Department of Biochemistry and Molecular Biology while working on her master of science degree, which she received in 1970, and her doctorate, which she received in 1973.

MARRIAGE AND FAMILY

During her rigorous routine of work and school, Lucid married and started a family. She and her husband, Michael, met in 1967 and married in 1968. Their first daughter, Kawai Dawn, was born in 1969. Kawai is named after the spot in Hawaii where Shannon and Michael spent their honeymoon. Another daughter, Shandara, was born in 1970, and a son, Michael, was born in 1976.

One of her graduate school professors remembers Lucid coming in to take a test the day after Shandara was born. "What are you doing here?" he asked. "I've studied hard for this exam, and I'm not going to study for it again," Lucid replied.

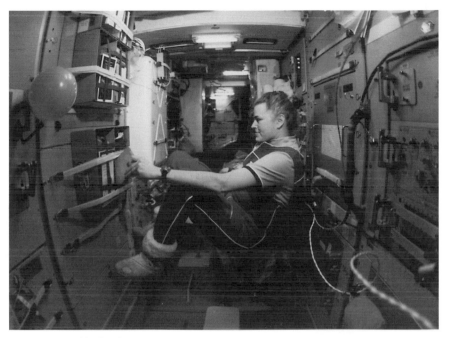

Lucid floating in space aboard the Mir, a Russian space station

CAREER HIGHLIGHTS

After earning her doctorate from the University of Oklahoma in 1973, Lucid became a research associate with the Oklahoma Medical Research Foundation in Oklahoma City. She worked in that job for the next several years, researching the effect of cancer-causing agents on rats. Around this time, NASA—the National Aeronautics and Space Administration—announced that it was looking for new recruits for its astronauts program. And, for the first time in history, the program was open to women. Lucid leapt at the chance. She remembered too well her keen disappointment when the first NASA astronauts were selected in the 1960s. They were all men. "I couldn't believe it when they selected the first seven astronauts," she said. "I mean, it was incredible, the feeling of anger, because there were no females included in the selection. Even though they were all military people, that didn't justify anything. There was absolutely no reason not to have any females."

Starting to Work for NASA

In January 1978, Lucid was selected to be an astronaut. She was one of the first six women selected by NASA. Those first female astronauts included Sally Ride, the first woman astronaut to fly in space, and Judith Resnick, who died in the Challenger disaster in 1986. The woman trained just like the men.

They were spun around in a centrifuge to simulate space flight, dragged by motorcycles to mimic the drag of a parachute, and pried out of a small spacecraft forced to land in water. Lucid found it exhilarating.

As a pilot and a scientist, Lucid came to NASA with a broad range of experience. She is a "mission specialist," and is qualified to do a number of tasks. Over the past 12 years she has gone on five space missions and worked on an array of different experiments both in space and on the ground. She has done payload testing, shuttle testing, launch countdowns, as well as performing experiments for NASA's Shuttle Avionics Integration labs and the flight software labs. She has also served as spacecraft communicator at Mission Control in Houston for many space shuttle missions.

Missions in Space

Lucid first blasted off into space in 1985 aboard the space shuttle Discovery. During this seven-day mission she helped the crew release several communications satellites into space. While on board, the crew also performed x-ray astronomy experiments and biomedical experiments. The shuttle orbited the Earth 112 times during that mission, traveling 2.5 million miles in 169 hours.

Lucid's next space mission took place in October 1989. This time Lucid flew aboard the space shuttle Atlantis on a mission that launched the spacecraft Galileo on its journey to Jupiter. The crew also mapped the atmospheric ozone level, performed experiments on radiation and lightning, and studied how micro gravity effects plants. Over five days, Lucid and the crew of the Atlantis orbited the Earth 79 times, traveling 1.8 million miles in 119 hours.

In August 1991, Lucid traveled aboard the Atlantis again on a nine-day mission. After sending another satellite into space, Lucid and the crew performed numerous experiments in different areas of the physical, material, and life sciences. On this mission, the crew was particularly interested in gathering research for the planned Extended Duration Orbiter and Space Station Freedom. After orbiting the Earth 142 times and traveling 3.7 million miles in 213 hours, Lucid and the Atlantis crew returned to Earth.

Lucid's next flight took place in November 1993, aboard the space shuttle Columbia. This time the crew spent 14 days in space studying the physical effects of space travel on humans and animals. The crew performed experiments on themselves and on 48 rats they brought aboard. They tested the neurological, cardiovascular, metabolic, and musculoskeletal systems of humans and rats as they relate to space flight. The crew also performed engineering tests. According to NASA, this flight was one of the most successful and important in the agency's history. It also landed Lucid in the record books. After this mission, during which she orbited the Earth 225 times, and traveled 5.8 million miles in 336 hours, Lucid became the American woman with the most hours in space — 838 total hours.

Shannon Lucid would enter the history books again with her next mission, aboard the space station Mir.

Aboard the Mir

On March 22, 1996, Lucid took off from the Kennedy Space Center in Florida aboard the space shuttle Atlantis en route to the Russian space station Mir. The Mir is a Russian-built space craft that was launched 10 years ago by the Soviet Union. For years, throughout the Cold War, the U.S. and the Soviet Union were engaged in a highly competitive space race. But with the breakup of the Soviet Union and the downfall of its Communist government, relations between the U.S. and Russia have improved. Over the past several years, the Russians have invited NASA astronauts to live and work aboard the Mir.

The Mir is a rather large space station that is made up of seven modules that have been put together over the past 10 years to form a "home" of some 13,000 feet of living space. There are separate areas for engineering and scientific experiments, as well as eating, sleeping, and exercising, and each astronaut has private quarters. The astronauts have sleeping quarters in a small, curtained area. Because water is so scarce, they make do with sponge baths and shampoo with a gel that is toweled off.

———— " ————

Lucid was extremely disappointed in the 1960s, when NASA selected only men to be the first astronauts. "I couldn't believe it when they selected the first seven astronauts. I mean, it was incredible, the feeling of anger, because there were no females included in the selection. Even though they were all military people, that didn't justify anything. There was absolutely no reason not to have any females."

———— " ————

The Mir circles the Earth continuously. Astronauts reach the Mir by way of a space shuttle, which docks with the Mir in space. The crew members change every four months or so. Shipments of supplies are also regularly sent to Mir, as are any parts that might need repair or replacement.

Lucid was aboard the Mir with two Russians cosmonauts, both named Yuri. At first it seemed as if there might be a bit of cultural complication between the Russians and their American counterpart. When interviewed prior to Lucid's arrival on Mir, the "two Yuris," as she called them, said they were happy to have a woman aboard, because "we know women love to clean."

The Mir

But Lucid, known for her good humor as well as her sense of camaraderie, ignored the sexist implications. By all reports, she got along very well with the Yuris. At one point, she mentioned that whenever the Russian cosmonauts went for a spacewalk, "Yuri takes a big piece of red tape and puts it across the communications controls I am absolutely not to touch." Yet this action didn't make her angry; she said that she would have done the same thing, if their roles had been reversed.

Lucid's scientific mission on the Mir included a number of experiments, some 35 in all. In one experiment, she studied how protein crystals grow in space; in another, she investigated how quail embryos develop in zero gravity. She also grew dwarf wheat and studied its progress. If astronauts someday travel as far as Mars, they will need to grow food in space. Lucid observed how the growth of wheat is effected by micro gravity.

Another experiment involved studying how combustion is effected by lack of gravity. For this experiment, Lucid lit birthday candles and measured the flames. The candles burned for up to 45 minutes (they burn for about one minute in Earth's gravity). Also, the flame was a small blue dot, and it emitted no smoke. This test will help in fire prevention in space.

Lucid felt she could have handled even more experiments. "I know many times investigators hear astronauts say 'time is very valuable and you need to make your experiments without much astronaut involvement'. But I would say the opposite—especially for space station long-duration flights. The thing that's really interesting is when you can get involvement in an experiment and make observations to help the investigators [on the ground] come to conclusions."

Lucid remained in close contact with a NASA science crew that was based in Moscow. Their communication and ability to rely on one another to guarantee the success of the experiments were an important part of the mission's success. According to Lucid, "A good example is a Canadian experiment where they were trying to isolate a materials payload from the micro gravity environment to get an even better sample. They wanted to send data down the real time to help change their software program. But we were having some downlink problems getting the raw data transmitted. But on board Mir we were able to analyze the data, get the graphs from the on board computer and use the downlink television to video the information down. Then using that, the investigator and ground team were able to suggest changes in the software to improve the experiment."

While she was on the Mir, the space station was updated with a final segment, called the Priroda, which was a module containing a lab for science experiments. "Priroda" is the Russian word for nature, and it included sensors that would study the Earth during Mir orbits. The Priroda was dropped off by a shuttle and traveled through space to be attached to the Mir. Lucid remembered that "As a graduate student years ago, I fantasized about having my own laboratory. I must admit, though, that in none of my fantasies was I gazing out the window of a space station watching 'my laboratory' approach like a gigantic silver bullet moving in slow motion toward the station's heart! Reality is indeed stranger than fiction!"

As the three astronauts worked to install the Priroda, they were surrounded by batteries, scrap metal and tools floating around them. "Periodically, free-floating metal pieces would impact each other creating clear metallic tones like cathedral bells in the module, and we joked with each other about the "cosmic music" that we were hearing," Lucid remembered.

"Pink Socks and Jello"

Lucid stayed in touch with her family through daily e-mail, sent from Mir via space satellite to her home in Houston. She also sent several letters home via e-mail that show her vivacious humor and sense of fun. One letter is entitled "Pink Socks and Jello." In the letter, Lucid describes how they keep track of time in space, where they don't have regular, 24-hour days defined by the rising and setting of the sun."When light follows darkness every 45 minutes, it is important that I have simple ways of marking the passage of time," she wrote. One way she did that was by wearing pink socks and eating Jello every

Sunday. Lucid called the Jello "the greatest improvement in space flight since my first flight over 10 years ago. When I found out that there was a refrigerator on board Mir, I asked the food folks at Johnson Space Center if they would put Jello in a drink bag. Once aboard Mir, we could just add hot water, put the bag in the refrigerator and, later, have a great treat. Well, the food folks did just that and sent a variety of flavors with me to try out. We tried the Jello first as a special treat for Easter. It was so great that we decided the crew tradition would be to share a bag of Jello every Sunday night. Every once in a while, Yuri will come up to me and say, "Isn't today Sunday?" and I will say "No, it's not. No Jello tonight!!!"

With letters like this coming out of Mir, Lucid became a favorite of the people and the press back on Earth. Once, she e-mailed that she was having a "crisis"—she'd run out of M & Ms. Over the six months she stayed on board Mir, the crew received several shipments from home, with letters, healthy food, and some junk food—including M & Ms and potato chips—for Lucid. One shipment brought fresh tomatoes, which the astronauts loved. "For the next week we had fresh tomatoes three times a day," wrote Lucid. "It was a sad meal when we ate the last ones!!!"

That same shipment brought new books to read. "My daughters had hand-selected each one, so I knew I'd enjoy them. I picked up one and rapidly read it. I came to the last page and the hero, who was being chased by an angry mob, escaped by stepping through a mirror. The end. Continued in Volume Two. And was there Volume Two in my book bag? No. Could I dash out to the bookstore? No. Talk about a feeling of total isolation and frustration!!!" Despite her disappointment, Lucid valued all the books and e-mail letters from home. They helped to overcome the feelings of loneliness and boredom that sometimes plague astronauts on long missions. In addition to reading, the astronauts watched movies. A favorite was *Apollo 13*, in both the English and the Russian versions.

Lucid remembers looking out the window at the Earth. One night, "there were thunderstorms out in the Atlantic, with a brilliant display of lightening like visual tom toms. The cities were strung out like Christmas lights along the coast." And she loved to watch the seasons change out her window. "One of the really neat things about having a long flight is that I've been able to see the seasons change over the Earth," she said. "When I launched in March, the northern part of Earth was covered with snow and ice and I got to see the ice in all the lakes breakup and then I got to see the Earth green."

One of the serious concerns about extended space flight is the effect of weightlessness on the human body. Without gravity, blood pools in the upper part of the body, and the heart beats with less strength. The bones lose calcium, and muscles atrophy. To counteract these effects, Lucid spent two hours every day running on a treadmill. Because she was weightless, she had to at-

Lucid aboard the Mir

tach herself to the treadmill with a bungee cord. Even though it was boring, and she swears she never wants to see another treadmill, her workouts paid off. Unlike other astronauts who lost significant weight and muscle in space, Lucid returned from six months in space in excellent physical shape.

Leaving the Mir

When Lucid began her mission in March 1996, she was supposed to return that August, after about five months in space. But in August, NASA reported having problems with the booster rockets of the shuttle that was supposed to pick her up. Then, when that problem was solved, a hurricane moved into Cape Canaveral, Florida, where the shuttle takes off. All together, she was delayed returning to Earth by about one month. The space shuttle Atlantis finally lifted off on its mission to bring Lucid back to Earth in September. As a special incentive, Lucid asked mission control in Houston to play Fontella Bass's 1960s hit "Rescue Me" to inspire the crew. The Atlantis docked with the Mir, and a smiling Lucid greeted her crew and welcomed her American replacement.

Returning to Earth on September 26, 1996, Lucid entered the record books, completing a mission in which she traveled 75.2 million miles in 188 days, the longest space mission of any American astronaut, and the record for a woman in space. And to the surprise of the medical team that met her, Lucid was in such great shape that she was able to walk off the shuttle. After meeting with her family, she took part in a round of physical tests to determine the effects of six months of weightlessness and travel in space. So far, it looks as if her exercise regimen kept her in good cardiovascular and muscular health.

Life Back on Earth

Lucid was surprised and delighted by the throngs of people who welcomed her back to Earth. President Clinton greeted her with a two-pound box of M & Ms, wrapped in a gold box. She received 188 pounds of Lay's potato chips. Her hometown gave her a parade, and a local elementary school presented her with a quilt with aliens stitched on it.

—————— **"** ——————

"One of the really neat things about having a long flight is that I've been able to see the seasons change over the Earth. When I launched in March, the northern part of Earth was covered with snow and ice and I got to see the ice in all the lakes breakup and then I got to see the Earth green."

—————— **"** ——————

Lucid was delighted to be with her family again, and looked forward to some "gooey desserts" and a hot shower when she finally reached home. But while her kids had missed their mom, they didn't necessarily miss her cooking. Michael celebrated his 21st birthday and Shandara her 26th birthday while Lucid was in space, and some of the media asked the Lucid kids if they missed their mom's special cooking for their birthday dinners. Shandara got a puzzled look on her face, then told the reporters that her mom's best meal was Domino's pizza.

Shannon Lucid continues to be an inspiration to children all over the country, particularly girls. As one middle school teacher wrote to Lucid: "I cannot tell you how important your work has been for all females involved in science. My students will benefit from your example. Thanks for being brave and bold. We love you!"

HOBBIES AND OTHER INTERESTS

Lucid enjoys camping and hiking out in the countryside, and she still likes to fly. She also likes to rollerblade, shop in bookstores, and read. But she hasn't yearned for a walk on the treadmill since she returned from space.

As for future plans, Lucid says she would love to be part of the first mission to Mars.

HONORS AND AWARDS

Congressional Space Medal of Honor (U.S. Congress): 1997
Order of Friendship Award (Russian Government): 1997

FURTHER READING

Books

Who's Who of American Women, 1997-98

Periodicals

Aviation Week and Space Technology, Sep. 30, 1996, p.26
Christian Science Monitor, Oct. 25, 1996, p.A1
Houston Chronicle, Sep. 27, 1996, p.A1; Dec. 3, 1996, p.A9
Los Angeles Times, Dec. 8, 1996, p.A3
New York Times, Sep. 16, 1996, p.A11; Sep. 17, 1996, p.C7; Sep. 19, 1996, p.A1; Sep. 21, 1996, p.A6; Sep. 24, 1996, p.A23; Sep. 27, 1996, p.A1; Oct. 25, 1996, p.A22
Newsweek, Sep. 30, 1996, p.68; Oct. 7, 1996, p.31
People, Feb. 6, 1978, p.30; July 22, 1996, p.36; Dec. 30, 1996, p.88
Time, Sep. 30, 1996, p.63
USA Today, Sep. 26, 1996, p.A4
U.S. News and World, Feb. 23, 1981, p.60; Oct. 7, 1996, p.9
Washington Post, Aug. 30, 1996, p.A1; Sep. 29, 1996, p.A3; Oct. 25, 1996, p.A12

ADDRESS

NASA
Lyndon B. Johnson Space Center
Houston, TX 77058

WORLD WIDE WEB SITE

http:www.jsc.nasa.gov/Bios/htmlbios/lucid.html

Margaret Mead 1901-1978

American Anthropologist and Ethnographer
Author of *Coming of Age in Samoa*

BIRTH

Margaret Mead was born on December 16, 1901, in Philadelphia, Pennsylvania. Her mother, Emily Fogg Mead, was a teacher and sociologist, and her father, Edward Sherwood Mead, was an economics professor at the University of Pennsylvania. Margaret was the oldest of their five children, although only four survived childhood: Margaret, Richard (born 1904), Elizabeth (1909), and Priscilla (1911). One sister, Catherine, died nine months after her birth in 1907.

YOUTH

Margaret Mead's life was anything but conventional. Her father's job at the University of Pennsylvania involved establishing different extension programs around the state, so the family moved frequently. Mead once estimated that she lived in 60 different homes by the time she reached her teenage years. Her father perfectly fit the absent-minded professor image. He had hoped for a son when Margaret was born and later told her, "It's a pity you aren't a boy; you'd have gone far."

While Mead respected her father, she received direction and nurturing from her mother, Emily Mead, and her grandmother, Martha Ramsay Mead. Margaret deeply admired both women. At a time when most women were confined to the household, they had attended college and balanced careers with family responsibilities. Her mother encouraged the children to read and think for themselves and surrounded them with books and other intellectual pursuits. A staunch opponent of bigotry and an avid supporter of equal rights for women, Emily Mead urged her children to play with children of other backgrounds in an effort to prevent prejudice. Later in life she encouraged her daughters to retain their maiden names after marriage so as to preserve their individuality.

Mead learned how to observe people's behavior very early. In her family, the women kept notebooks on one another. Her grandmother recorded the grandchildren's emotional life, while her mother recorded their intellectual development. From them Margaret learned to observe everything around her. At age eight, she was set to work watching her younger sisters, scribbling notes on their speech habits in a notebook.

Mead showed flashes of her strong individuality at an early age. When she was three, her father took her to Philadelphia where he pretended to abandon her because she misbehaved. Rather than wail for her absent father, Mead shouted so that passersby could hear, "Bad Dada to go off and leave his poor little baby girl!" Embarrassed, her father had to emerge from hiding and re-claim his child in front of the angry glares of onlookers. Eight years later Mead developed a strong religious sense. On her own initiative, she was baptized in the Episcopalian Church. Her parents, who never placed much value on orga-nized religion, were surprised at the action but also impressed that such a young person would take such a huge step. Her father even teased Margaret about this, and whenever she did something he did not like he chided that he would have her "unbaptized." She remained a devout Episcopalian through-out her life.

While Mead flourished under this unusual upbringing, she also yearned for the things that other girls her age had. Current fashions appealed to her more than the sensible, unattractive clothing that her mother selected for her. In spite of this Mead appreciated the foundation her parents and grandmother tried to instill and refused to follow the crowd just to be accepted. As she said, "I also wanted to be very sure that I would always be recognized as myself."

EDUCATION

Mead experienced little formal education while she was growing up. Her parents and grandmother strongly disapproved of the typically rigid manner of teaching, which forced students to remain at their desks all day memorizing useless information. After kindergarten, Mead spent only one year—the fourth grade—in a regular school before she reached high school. Instead her grandmother, who had been a school teacher and principal and believed that learning came from experiencing things, tutored Mead and her brother and sisters for an hour each day, then sent them out to the fields to observe nature or to a library for research.

> *Mead wrote that her grandmother "thought that memorizing mere facts was not very important and that drill was stultifying. The result was that I was not well drilled in geography or spelling. But I learned to observe the world around me and to note what I saw."*

Mead wrote that her grandmother "thought that memorizing mere facts was not very important and that drill was stultifying. The result was that I was not well drilled in geography or spelling. But I learned to observe the world around me and to note what I saw." Later in life Mead would affirm that her grandmother was "the most decisive influence in my life. She had gone to college when this was a very unusual thing for a girl to do, she had a firm grasp of anything she paid attention to, she had married and had a child, and she had a career of her own."

While Mead's grandmother organized field trips to local museums and zoos, her mother hired artisans to visit their home and teach the children carpentry, wood carving, or clay modeling. Mead excelled in this unorthodox style of education, in which she could indulge her inquisitive nature to her heart's content.

College Years at DePauw University

In 1919 Mead excitedly awaited the start of her freshman year at DePauw University in Indiana, where she thought she would begin serious study of important topics and would "stay up all night talking about things that mattered." Instead, she quickly became a social outcast. A sorority invited Mead to join their group, but the girls quickly changed their minds. When they interviewed Mead they refused to admit her because she did not dress in the current fashions, she spoke with an eastern accent, and she preferred studying to having a wild time. For the first time Mead felt the sting of bigotry and vowed that she would battle it whenever possible.

She gravitated toward several other "socially unacceptable" girls, with whom she formed a loosely organized group as a way of thumbing their noses at the sorority system. Proudly calling themselves "The Minority," Mead's gathering included an African-American, a Catholic, and the only Jewish student on campus.

Mead experienced another form of bigotry in the classroom, where her impressive intellectual skills propelled her to the top of her class. This success only turned her into a target for the more jealous students, especially males. She concluded that while "bright girls could do better than bright boys," because of resentment they "would suffer for it." Mead battled this unfair treatment for much of her life.

Transferring to Barnard College

Mead was so disillusioned with DePauw that in 1920 she switched to Barnard College, an all-female school in New York City that was associated with Columbia University. Here she found the intellectual stimulation and challenge she had hoped to discover in Indiana. Before long she was involved in a wide variety of campus activities, including editing the school newspaper.

Though she had no idea which field she wanted to enter, Mead at first believed she would become either a painter or a writer. However, in her senior year she took a class in anthropology offered by Dr. Franz Boas, one of the world's ranking anthropologists, and his graduate assistant, Ruth Benedict, who also became a leader in the field. At that time, anthropology in this country was a developing science, and Boas is credited with providing the scientific foundation for a whole generation of American anthropologists.

Boas and Benedict believed that the best way to study ancient civilizations was not to unearth artifacts or conduct statistical analysis. They preferred field work, which at that time was highly unusual. They studied life in primitive cultures in isolated and remote areas, where the people were relatively untouched by modern society. Boas and Benedict were in a race against time, trying to study such groups before modern civilization eradicated all traces of their traditional customs. By studying these societies, Boas and Benedict believed they could answer questions about the nature of human behavior. For example, they could study differing expectations for men and women, or the way children are raised. Understanding how other cultures address these issues could shed light on our own society, to explain whether our attitudes and behavior result from human nature or from social conditioning. Boas and Benedict explained to Mead the urgent need to study these primitive cultures before they disappeared, telling her they had "nothing to offer but an opportunity to do work that matters."

Mead was hooked. She had located her life's work, telling family members that "Anthropology has to be done now. Other things can wait." Since anthropology was a predominantly male-dominated field, Mead decided to focus on an area that few of her male colleagues bothered to examine—families and child-rearing practices.

Mead earned her bachelor of arts degree (B.A.) from Barnard in 1923. That same year, she married theology student Luther Cressman, the first of Mead's three husbands, and entered the school of anthropology at Columbia University. She earned her master of arts degree (M.A.) from Columbia under Dr. Boas the following year. In 1925 she completed the work for her Ph.D., writing a thesis called "An Inquiry into the Question of Cultural Stability in Polynesia." After spending the next several years doing field work, she received her doctorate (Ph.D.) in anthropology in 1929 from Columbia University.

CAREER HIGHLIGHTS

Margaret Mead is considered one of the pioneers in the field of anthropology. In a career that spanned over 50 years, she was active in field work, as a writer, as a teacher, as a lecturer, and as a museum curator. Today, Mead is considered an ethnographer or cultural anthropologist, one who records, analyzes, and compares various human cultures. She based her life's work on her studies of seven groups of people from the South Pacific: the Samoan, Manus (sometimes spelled Manua), Arapesh, Mundugumor, Tchambuli, Iatmul, and Balinese. But she is perhaps best known for her early work in the Samoan Islands.

Field Work in Samoa

In 1925, Mead was ready to complete her first field work. She planned to work among some of the tribes native to the South Pacific. But Boas was worried for her safety, afraid to send such a young woman to such an inaccessible and primitive place. He argued that she should select a more secure location. Mead told her father that Boas was trying to force her to study a group she did not want, so her father offered to assume the costs of the voyage. Boas, realizing he was beaten, convinced Mead to select the Samoan Islands, which were under the jurisdiction of the United States Navy and thus offered some semblance of security and order.

Mead displaying some trophy heads from head-hunting tribes in New Guinea, 1934

Mead faced outright sexism and discrimination throughout her career. Before she left the United States some anthropologists, all male, criticized her for attempting field work. One bluntly told her that she should stay home and have children rather than travel to distant lands to study them. Mead understood that she would often face such remarks and ignored the rude suggestion.

Mead left for Samoa with a specific goal. In her field work there, she was most interested in the behavior of adolescent girls. She hoped to answer one major question—whether "the disturbances which vex our adolescents [are] due to the nature of adolescence itself or the civilization." In other words, she intended to find out if the behavior and traumatic changes experienced by youth were common to people in all societies, or if they were caused by society itself.

Mead's Methods

In 1925 she packed her necessities—a typewriter, a flashlight, a few clothes, and a metal strongbox in which to place her notes—and boarded a San Francisco steamer headed to Hawaii. After a brief stay in the Hawaiian

Islands, where she studied Polynesian grammar, Mead boarded a second steamer for the lengthy voyage to Samoa. When she arrived, Mead spent six weeks staying in a hotel so she could learn the language and customs of the people she intended to study. She then spent eight months living in three different coastal villages on the island of Tau.

In Samoa, Mead developed the methods she would use for doing research on various cultures throughout her life. Mead's methods were revolutionary. She asserted that "the only way in which I could be sure of knowing how a Samoan girl acted was to try to act that way myself." She tried to blend in with the Samoans, "speaking their language, eating their food, sitting cross-legged on the pebbly floor." In Samoa Mead lived among the natives in the village, learned their local customs and languages, helped care for the children, and ate such foods as wild boar and wild pigeon. In this way, she gained the confidence of the people. Natives marveled at her ability to sit on the ground for hours without moving, just taking extensive notes as events unfolded. As one colleague commented, "She knows how to use her eyes, how to see. She has an uncanny perception for different cultural styles." One of her most profound traits as an anthropologist, according to many, was her ability to shed cultural preconceptions from Western society.

— " —

Mead's methods were revolutionary. She asserted that "the only way in which I could be sure of knowing how a Samoan girl acted was to try to act that way myself."
She tried to blend in with the Samoans, "speaking their language, eating their food, sitting cross-legged on the pebbly floor."

— " —

Coming of Age in Samoa

Mead's findings about the Samoan people would prove to be controversial. She described Samoan society as gentle, easy, and casual, marked by loose family ties, no guilt, no violence, and no conflict. She concluded that Samoan society, unlike that of the United States, placed few restrictions or pressures upon its youth, especially in the area of sex. As a result, young people in Samoa matured without the feelings of guilt and stress that plagued American youth and avoided much of the turbulence that American teenagers experienced. The obvious conclusion, in her opinion, was that culture had a far stronger influence on the development of personality than heredity, as most anthropologists then believed. And her conclusion implied that American culture, in particular, was at fault for the difficulties experienced by American youth.

Mead summarized all of this in her first book, *Coming of Age in Samoa* (1928), which was completely different from other anthropological books of its time. It was descriptive rather than statistical, written in an easy-going style that avoided the stilted prose of other anthropology books. In fact, it read like a novel, with characters drawn from Samoan society. Soon, *Coming of Age in Samoa* soared to the top of the best-seller lists. Younger Americans, already drawn to the liberated lifestyle of the "Roaring Twenties," responded to Mead's message of greater sexual freedom and less social pressure. The book attracted many young people to the field of anthropology, and before long it rose to be the best-selling anthropology book of all time.

Though she had made a profound impact on her field, Mead suffered from biting criticism. As Winthrop Sargeant wrote in the *New Yorker* magazine, "The very features that made *Coming of Age in Samoa* popular with the general public—its clarity and its insistence on the role of anthropology as a source of improving lessons for the civilized world—were regarded by some anthropologists as unorthodox and scientifically impure." One source of criticism was her method of living among and interacting with the natives, called the participant observer method. While it produced impressive results, it was also criticized by some anthropologists, who contended that scientists should never become involved with their subjects, only study them. Critics also called the book subjective and lacking in verifiable data that could be statistically analyzed. Unlike other anthropologists who relied entirely upon such statistical data, Mead applied her knowledge of other sciences to her study. She used physiology, ecology, nutrition, and psychology to help formulate her conclusions. Finally, Mead upset some members of her profession by refusing to simply record her observations on Samoan culture. Instead, she compared child-rearing practices and the role of women in Samoa and America and suggested changes that her country should make.

After her stay in Samoa, Mead returned to the United States to complete her doctoral degree. She also became assistant curator of ethnology at the American Museum of Natural History in New York City, where she was affiliated throughout her life. For Mead, her goal in working at the museum was "to make Americans understand cultural anthropology as well as they understood archeology." She also began amassing the extensive collection of cultural artifacts that she would eventually donate to the museum.

Field Work in New Guinea

In 1928-29, Mead returned to the South Pacific to study a different group of villagers. In conjunction with her second husband, the New Zealand anthropologist Reo Fortune, she worked with the Manus people, a fishing and trading tribe from the Admirality Islands off the coast of New Guinea. Once again living with the natives, this time in a thatched roof house on stilts, Mead earned such enormous respect from the villagers that they called her *pilapen*, which meant female chief. When she departed, the Manus men played the death roll on their drums.

On her return to the U.S., she published *Growing Up in New Guinea* (1930). Here, she detailed many of the customs of the Manus, which she described as a formal, strict, and individualistic people. They revered success, they used commerce, and they had no feeling for romance and no love songs or poetry. They also reversed what Americans then considered the normal sex roles in the family setting, with the mother as the stern, aloof disciplinarian and the father as the more loving, forgiving, and understanding parent. Because these parental roles differed so much from the American approach at that time, Mead used her findings as an opportunity to examine sex roles and their effect on the development of children's attitudes. About 25 years later, Mead returned to the same village to find the community going through a difficult transition to modern life. She discussed this transition in *New Lives for Old* (1956).

After briefly studying a Native-American tribe in Nebraska in 1929, Mead spent much of the next several years living among various tribal groups in New Guinea, including the Arapesh, Mundugumor, and Tchambuli tribes. Her purpose in contrasting these three tribes was to study the "conditioning of social personalities of the two sexes." The first tribe, the Arapesh, were peaceable, humor-loving, cooperative, non-aggressive, and devoted to family life. They lived according to the belief that "all people are good and gentle, that men and women alike are neither strongly nor aggressively sexed, that no one has any other motive except to grow yams and children." In contrast, the second tribe, the Mundugumor, were a vicious tribe of cannibals and headhunters whose whole social structure was built on hostility. They hated gentleness of any kind, even toward children. Though the New Guinea government had outlawed cannibalism three years before Mead and Fortune arrived, they took extra precautions by permitting no more than three villagers into their hut at any one time. The third tribe, the Tchambuli, practiced ceremonial head-hunting, but they were not very warlike. In their tribes, the social power was held by the women, who were happy, independent, and somewhat rough. The men, who were more emotional, tended to be great actors and artists.

Mead recorded her findings about New Guinea's tribes in *Sex and Temperament in Three Primitive Societies* (1935), which examined how these different societies defined acceptable behavior standards for males and females. As Winthrop Sargeant summarized Mead's findings for the *New Yorker*, "The three tribes provided Dr. Mead with an excellent laboratory for comparisons of radically different systems of behavior of the sexes. The Arapesh ideal seemed to consist of a mild, responsive man married to a mild,

Visiting the Admirality Islands in 1953

responsive woman; the Mundugumor ideal, of a violent, aggressive man married to a violent, aggressive woman; and the Tchambuli ideal, of a dominant, impersonal, managing woman married to an irresponsible, emotionally dependent man." Because of the vast differences among the men and women of these three tribes, Mead concluded that emotional and behavioral characteristics do not result from one's sex, but instead result from social conditioning. "Human nature," she declared, "is almost unbelievably malleable." While her conclusions were certainly controversial, *Sex and Temperament in Three Primitive Societies* established Mead as one of the nation's foremost anthropologists. Written in the smooth-flowing prose that had captivated the American public earlier in *Coming of Age in Samoa*, it further helped to popularize her field and solidified her professional reputation as an anthropologist.

Mead's Field Work in Bali and Her Use of Photography

Between 1936 and 1939, Mead also did extensive field work on the island of Bali. She was working at the time with her third husband, the English anthropologist Gregory Bateson, whom she married during this period. Tourists had always described Bali as an island paradise, filled with happy and carefree people. Mead found it very different. She characterized the Balinese as a society of schizophrenics dominated by fear. That fear was demonstrated in the society's ritualistic ceremonies, which the Balinese viewed as a guarantee of safety. Mead also found that the schizophrenia was deliberately cultivated in infancy. Balinese mothers would methodically frustrate their children, who would gradually give up all hope of maternal affection and would retreat into a dream world. Trance and other types of dissociative behavior were common throughout Balinese society.

While studying the people of Bali, Mead and Bateson made a side trip in 1938. They went to New Guinea to study the Iatmul tribe, a people living in villages along the banks of the Sepik River. There, they built a house without walls so that they could quietly observe everything that went on around them. They found that fishing and caring for the sago palm tree, a source of starch for both food and textiles, were the Iatmul peoples' main support—and both were the responsibility of women.

One of Mead's most important contributions of the 1930s was the use of photography and film to record various cultures. Up to that point anthropologists didn't use photography to document their work. In Bali and New Guinea, Mead and Bateson shot over 25,000 photographs, including 752 photos that were published in their joint study *Balinese Character* (1942). By using film, it became possible to record and analyze behavioral characteristics that would be missed by an anthropologist relying only on notes. Ever since, the technique has become a common practice in the field. As *Time* magazine recalled, "She was one of the first anthropologists to use still and motion pictures to record the customs and habits of primitive societies. She was also one of the first to develop the subscience of semiotics, or the study of how men communicate by gestures."

Later Work

From 1939-1945 World War II interrupted Mead's field work in the South Pacific. While that struggle continued, she worked for the United States government devising ways to study cultures at a distance, particularly that of the nation's enemies, Germany and Japan. She used movies, fiction, and interviews with people who had come from those nations to gather valuable data. Mead also chaired the Committee on Food Habits, a group that produced suggestions for the country about how people could cope with the food shortages caused by war.

In the 1950s and 1960s Mead revisited many of the villages of the South Pacific she had studied earlier and received warm welcomes. One tribe, the Iatmul, met her at the dock as her ship approached, serenaded her with "My Darling Clementine," then carried her to their village. However, by that point other pursuits had begun to occupy more of her time.

A Flourishing Writing and Speaking Career

In the later part of her career, Mead devoted less time to field studies and more time to writing, producing best-selling and influential works on anthropology. In 1942 she published *And Keep Your Powder Dry: An Anthropologist Looks at America*, which analyzed American society in relation to the seven tribal cultures that she had studied over the years. Seven years later, in *Male and Female* (1949), Mead examined the different expectations that society placed on men and women, and their different characteristics, to determine if their different attitudes and behaviors resulted from biological determinism or social conditioning. In it, she observed that "Differences in sex as they are known today are based on the bringing up by the mother—she is always pushing the female toward similarity and the male toward difference." *Culture and Commitment: A Study of the Generation Gap* (1970) is considered her most theoretical book—and also one of her most satisfying. It presented a closely reasoned argument about different types of cultures. She described the U.S. as moving from one type to another, one in which the ideas and experiences of younger people predominated. She writes about some of the critical events of that era—changes in morals, confusion over sex roles, fear about the atom bomb, environmental degradation, the influence of television—and says that "all these have brought about a drastic, irreversible division between the generations." In her 1972 autobiography, *Blackberry Winter: My Earlier Years*, Mead described both her personal life and her professional experiences in Samoa and elsewhere in the warm, engaging style that her fans had come to love. As Arthur Cooper wrote in *Newsweek*, "Finally, at 70, anthropologist Mead has decided to tell us about Mead the woman, and she does it with typical grace in her customary clear, jargon-free prose. To read this book is to enjoy a moveable and very moving feast."

> *"Differences in sex as they are known today are based on the bringing up by the mother—she is always pushing the female toward similarity and the male toward difference."*

In addition to her many books, Mead wrote hundreds of articles for newspapers, magazines, and scholarly journals. In 1961 she began a series of articles for the popular magazine, *Redbook*, in which she gave her views on subjects ranging from education and family life to national character.

When not writing, Mead delivered as many as 100 lectures each year. A fluent speaker with an amazing memory for facts, she delivered her speeches without notes. Clutching her "thumbstick," a walking stick from New Guinea she

*Mead in the Hall of the Peoples of the Pacific at the
Museum of Natural History, 1971*

used because of lingering effects from a broken ankle, she spoke to packed audiences on an amazingly wide variety of subjects. In fact, officials at the American Museum of Natural History once compiled a list of topics in which Mead was considered an expert. The 12 areas included education and culture, mental health, national character, and ecology. After one lecture about tribal customs, a spectator asked Mead a question about the use of betel nuts in the Admiralty Islands. She quickly embarked upon a lengthy answer that stunned listeners with its thoroughness. Her speeches often made colleagues uneasy because, as one mentioned, "You wonder what she'll take off on next. We know what Dr. Blank will say—he's probably already distributed his paper. But we're never sure about Margaret Mead."

During the last 25 years of her life Mead taught at numerous colleges, including Vassar, Stanford, Fordham, and her favorite, Columbia. Her popular classes, which quickly filled with students, reflected her broad areas of interest. In 1966, for example, she taught three courses—"Cultures of the Pacific," "Methods and Problems in Anthropology," and "Culture and Personality."

An activity dear to Mead's heart was her work with the American Museum of Natural History in New York City. From 1926 until 1969 she held the positions of assistant curator, curator, and curator emeritus. In 1971 she opened the museum's Hall of the Peoples of the Pacific, to which she contributed her priceless collection of the artifacts and records she had gathered over a lifetime of work. She also started the Institute for Intercultural Studies, a foundation that assists young men and women who hope to enter the field of anthropology. Mead donated a huge portion of her book earning to this foundation. Besides this work, Mead served as president of three organizations—the World Federation of Mental Health from 1956-1957, the American Anthropological Association in 1960, and the American Association for the Advancement of Science in 1975.

Mead's Later Years

Mead's major interests evolved during her career. While in her early years she hurried to study individual cultures before they disappeared, in the 1960s and 1970s her concern broadened to the entire world. She began to take a holistic approach to world culture and the individual's place in it. Her concerns reflected her longing to create "from a hundred cultures, one culture which does what no culture has ever done before—gives a place to every human gift." Mead believed that the alarming spread of nuclear weapons and the destruction of the environment placed every human being in danger. She devoted much of her efforts to combating these two evils. She bemoaned the incredible pressures placed upon modern families and the virtual disappearance in American society of the extended family.

Mead was also concerned about society's unequal treatment of females. Women were either confined to the home or, if they chose a career, became the subject of verbal abuse and jealousy from male colleagues. Mead claimed that "we end up with the contradiction of a society that appears to throw the doors open to women, but translates her every step toward success as having been damaging." The *New York Times* called Mead the "general among the foot soldiers of modern feminism."

Mead's ideas found a ready audience among the generation growing up in the 1960s and 1970s, who responded to her advocacy of such controversial issues as legalizing marijuana and accepting greater sexual freedom. Mead contended that youth should have a greater say in the world's future. With the rapid advances in business and technology, their parents would not possess the knowledge to prepare them adequately. Consequently, younger people would have to create their own futures. "Children must be taught how to think, not what to think," she frequently asserted.

Final Days

Mead's feverish pace of work was so hectic that her first husband once remarked wistfully that he had to make an appointment to see her. Mead continued at that pace almost until her death. On her 75th birthday on December 16, 1976, a reporter asked if she planned to slow down. Mead smiled and replied, "I expect to die, but I don't plan to retire."

The next year she learned that she had pancreatic cancer, and she commenced on a year-long fight to beat the dreaded disease. Mead continued to work until physicians ordered her into a New York hospital, where she died on November 15, 1978.

In her honor, the American Museum of Natural History held a memorial service on January 20, 1979. In a show of enormous respect, so many co-workers and friends flooded the hall that many had to watch the proceedings on television in other rooms. The United States ambassador to the United Nations, Andrew Young, posthumously presented Mead with the nation's highest civilian peacetime award, the Presidential Medal of Freedom. He read President Jimmy Carter's words regretting Mead's loss and praising her extraordinary work, which had "brought the humane insights of cultural anthropology to a public of millions." Shortly after her death, the Manus people of New Guinea declared a week-long period of mourning and dispatched a telegram stating, "People sorry of Margaret Mead's death. With sympathy, respect. Rested seven days. Planted coconut tree memory of great friend."

Mead's Reputation and Her Legacy

Mead has been both criticized and exalted over the years. Her work was frequently dismissed as impressionistic and subjective, because she didn't rely exclusively on statistical information. She was criticized because her wide-ranging studies relied excessively on generalizations and failed to provide a broad theoretical interpretation of cultural behavior. Others, though, saw that as Mead's refusal to simplify what is by nature complex.

With time, though, that opinion began to change. "Mead slowly and surely began to assume the stature of one of the world's most important thinkers," Winthrop Sargeant wrote. "In purely scientific monographs, she proved over and over again that she could write as technically and obscurely as anyone else when she felt like it, but in her more popular works she kept up her crusade to bring anthropology home to the average educated reader and to convert it from a detached science into a practical tool for social therapy. Behind all her painstaking researches into primitive cultures in exotic jungles was the mind of a highly civilized woman, aware of world trends in politics, economics, psychology, and sociology, and anxious to bring her work to bear in a realistic way on the problems of the day."

Margaret Mead left a profound and enduring legacy. Her work influenced countless young students to enter the field of anthropology. She revolutionized the ways in which field research was conducted, moving beyond simple statistical analysis to draw on the disciplines of physiology, ecology, nutrition, economics, and psychology. In addition, her use of photography to expand her research base was also revolutionary. "Mead must be regarded as a pioneer whose innovations in research method have helped social anthropology to come of age as a science," Boyce Rensberger wrote in the *New York Times*.

> **"**
>
> *Boyce Rensberger wrote in the* **New York Times,** *"Mead must be regarded as a pioneer whose innovations in research method have helped social anthropology to come of age as a science."*
>
> **"**

Mead's work became the subject of a major controversy in 1983 with the publication of *Margaret Mead and Samoa: The Making and Unmaking of an Anthropological Myth* by Derek Freeman, an anthropologist who spent six years in Samoa off and on between 1940 and 1981. He disagreed fiercely with Mead on the nature of Samoan culture, saying it contained competition, crime, violence, aggression, and a sexual culture that valued virginity, not casual sex. He said that her conclusions were, "in reality, the figments of an anthropological myth." In Freeman's view, Mead created this myth because she was blinded by her belief in cultural determinism, the idea that a person's character is formed by social customs rather than innate tendencies. He also depicted her as young and innocent, lacking the life experience necessary for research in the field. His book set off a firestorm of controversy, with anthropologists lining up to support his claims or hers. Even Mead's supporters found some elements of his work to be believable. For example, they agreed she was young and inexperienced and may have been susceptible to misunderstanding. They also agreed that some underlying beliefs in her work, which may have been appropriate in the early part of this century, were no longer relevant by the 1980s. But for most commentators, these were minor issues that could not obscure Mead's enduring achievements.

"Mead's ethnography, awesomely meticulous as it was, may not be what saves her [reputation]," Jane Howard wrote in *Smithsonian* magazine. "An answer, as the Danish writer Isak Dineson once said, is a rarer thing than is commonly imagined. Maybe answers are not as important as is commonly imagined, either. Maybe questions matter more. And if Margaret Mead in her innocent early travels was guilty of some wrong answers, she kept on asking what many strongly feel were the right, the most urgent, questions. The question Ruth Bunzel says Mead took to Samoa was one she kept asking all her life: not 'How can we understand others?' but 'How can we understand ourselves?'"

MARRIAGE AND FAMILY

Mead was married three times. She married her first husband, theology student Luther Cressman, in 1923. To preserve her identity, she retained her name, which was so unusual at that time that many newspapers ran articles about it. She and Cressman were rarely together, as Mead was often out of the country. Their marriage was already in trouble in 1928, when Mead met New Zealand anthropologist Reo Fortune on the return boat trip from Samoa. The next year, she and Cressman were divorced, and then she and Fortune married. That union lasted eight years, during which they did several field studies together. In 1936 she divorced Fortune and married English anthropologist Gregory Bateson, whom she believed was the love of her life. Mead and Bateson also worked together on many field studies together, capturing their observations in film and photographs. In 1939, while married to Bateson, Mead gave birth to her only child, daughter Mary Catherine. In 1950 Mead and Bateson divorced. She remained single for the rest of her life.

Mead felt "women should not be forced to sacrifice all their talents as individuals in rearing children."

Mead raised her daughter, Mary Catherine, in an independent fashion. She felt strongly that "women should not be forced to sacrifice all their talents as individuals in rearing children," so she asked friends to look after her daughter while she conducted field work in the Pacific. Mead adopted the Samoan custom of raising children among large groups of other children, all surrounded by a community of adults to serve as substitute parents when needed.

Shortly after Mary Catherine was born, Mead and Bateson accepted an invitation to share a house in Greenwich Village, in New York City, with friends of the family, Lawrence Frank and his six children. Mary Catherine was raised there from age two to age 15, and she stayed with the Frank family when her mother was away. They spent their summers in New Hampshire, where they were surrounded by a large group of Mead's colleagues, psychologists, sociologists, and anthropologists.

SELECTED WRITINGS

Coming of Age in Samoa, 1928
Growing Up in New Guinea, 1930
Sex and Temperament in Three Primitive Societies, 1935
Balinese Character: A Photographic Analysis, (with Gregory Bateson), 1942
And Keep Your Powder Dry: An Anthropologist Looks at America, 1942
Male and Female: A Study of the Sexes in a Changing World, 1949
Growth and Culture: A Photographic Study of Balinese Childhoods, 1951
New Lives for Old, 1956
Continuities in Cultural Evolution, 1964
Culture and Commitment: A Study of the Generation Gap, 1970
Blackberry Winter: My Earlier Years, 1972
World Enough: Rethinking the Future, 1975
Letters from the Field, 1925-75, 1977

HONORS AND AWARDS

National Achievement Award (Chi Omega): 1940
Gold Medal Award (Society of Women Geographers): 1942
Viking Medal in anthropology: 1958
Outstanding Woman of the Year in Science (Associated Press): 1949
Medal of Honor (Rice University): 1962
Inducted into the Women's Hall of Fame (Nationwide Women Editors): 1965
William Proctor Prize for Scientific Achievement (Scientific Research Society
    of America): 1969
Arches of Science Award (Pacific Science Center): 1971
Kalinga Prize (UNESCO and government of India): 1971
Wilder Penfield Award (Vanier Institute of the Family): 1972
Lehmann Award (New York Academy of Sciences): 1973
Omega Achievers Award for Education: 1977
Presidential Medal of Freedom: 1979

FURTHER READING

Books

Bailey, Martha J. *American Women in Science*, 1994

Bateson, Mary Catherine. *With A Daughter's Eye: A Memoir of Margaret Mead and Gregory Bateson*, 1984

Church, Carol Bauer. *Margaret Mead: Student of the Global Village*, 1976 (juvenile)

Contemporary Authors New Revision Series, Vol. 4

Encyclopedia Britannica, 1995

Freeman, Derek. *Margaret Mead and Samoa: The Making and Unmaking of an Anthropological Myth*, 1983

Grolier Library of North American Biographies: Scientists, Vol. 8, 1994

Hammond, Allen L. *A Passion to Know*, 1984

Ludle, Jacqueline. *Margaret Mead*, 1983 (juvenile)

Magill, Frank N., editor. *Great Lives from History*, 1995

McGraw-Hill Encyclopedia of World Biography, Vol. 7, 1973

Mead, Margaret. *Blackberry Winter: My Earlier Years*, 1972

Peavy, Linda S. *Dreams Into Deeds*, 1985

Rice, Edward. *Margaret Mead: A Portrait*, 1979 (juvenile)

Stille, Darlene R. *Extraordinary Women Scientists*, 1995

Stoddard, Hope. *Famous American Women*, 1970

World Book Encyclopedia, 1997

Ziesk, Edra. *Margaret Mead*, 1990 (juvenile)

Periodicals

Current Biography Yearbook 1951; 1979 (obituary)

Life, May 1983, p.32

New Republic, Mar. 28, 1983, p.32

New York Times, Nov. 16, 1978, p.A1; January 31, 1983, p.A1

New York Times Book Review, Mar. 27, 1983, p.3; Aug. 26, 1984, p.1

New York Times Magazine, Apr. 26, 1970, p.23; Apr. 24, 1983, p.48

New Yorker, Dec. 30, 1961, p.31

Newsweek, Feb. 14, 1983, p.56

Scientific American, Nov. 1986, p.56

Smithsonian, Apr. 1983, p.66; Sep. 1984, p.118

Time, Feb. 14, 1983, p.68

Garrett Morgan 1877-1963

American Inventor and Businessman
Inventor of the Gas Mask and the Three-Way Traffic
Signal

BIRTH

Garrett Augustus Morgan was born March 4, 1877, on a farm in
the small town of Paris, Kentucky. He was the seventh of eleven
children born into a farming family headed by Sydney and
Elizabeth (Reed) Morgan.

YOUTH AND EDUCATION

Young Morgan's childhood was marked by poverty and hard

work. The entire region surrounding Paris was economically depressed, and his uneducated parents struggled to feed and clothe all their children on the modest income they were able to squeeze out of their farm. Since family finances were so tight, Morgan and his brothers and sisters helped out around the farm whenever they could.

But poverty was not the only problem that confronted the Morgan family. Black families like the Morgans often had to deal with racism from their white neighbors. Indeed, white people still enjoyed many economic and legal advantages over black people at the time. Slavery had been outlawed by President Abraham Lincoln's 1863 Emancipation Proclamation; in fact, Morgan's own mother had been freed by this proclamation just 14 years before his birth. Yet racism against black people was still particularly bad in America's Southern states, which had long supported slavery. Indeed, their support of slavery had led them to try to secede from the nation's Northern states and form their own country, called the Confederacy, in 1861. This decision angered America's Northern states, and in 1861 an armed conflict known as the Civil War erupted between the nation's Northern and Southern states. This devastating war lasted until 1865, when the North finally triumphed and restored the Union.

> *As his granddaughter Karen Morgan later recalled, Garrett Morgan "was a plain man . . . proud to be an American, proud of his race."*

Even though the war ended years before Morgan was born, its impact continued to be felt. During the Reconstruction era immediately following the Civil War, many white Southerners remained bitter about the outcome of the conflict. They made life miserable for the black families that lived among them. Although they were considered free, African-Americans lived in poverty, with few opportunities for jobs, miserable housing conditions, and no chance to get a good education.

Like many African-Americans at that time, Morgan had very little formal education. It was typical then for blacks to receive only an elementary school education, and he was no exception. At the age of 14, after completing fifth grade, he decided to set out on his own and build a new life for himself. With only a few coins in his pocket, he made his way north to Cincinnati, Ohio. The youngster knew that even though the North had successfully ended slavery in the United States, many of the people who lived in its cities and towns did not like blacks. But he decided that he would still have a better opportunity to build a good life for himself in a Northern town than he would in towns that had formerly flown the flag of the Confederacy.

Morgan found steady work as a handyman for a rich white landowner once he reached Cincinnati in 1891. The position did not pay very well, though, and after four years he left Cincinnati and moved to Cleveland, a city in northern Ohio that sits on the shores of Lake Erie. He did not know it at the time, but Cleveland would end up being his home for the rest of his life.

CAREER HIGHLIGHTS

Soon after arriving in Cleveland, Morgan found employment as a sewing machine mechanic and adjuster with a manufacturing company called Roots and McBridge. His supervisors soon discovered that he had an uncanny knack for fixing broken machinery. This talent allowed Morgan to secure jobs with several other Cleveland-area sewing machine companies during the next few years. It was also around this time that Morgan's inventive capabilities first became apparent. In 1901 he sold his first invention, a belt fastener for sewing machines, for $50.

In the years immediately following the sale of his first invention, Morgan's mechanical talents and developing business smarts made him a valuable employee, and he began to be paid accordingly. By 1907 he had saved enough money to open a shop that sold and repaired sewing machines. The store was immediately successful, and later that year Morgan was able to buy a house. Within weeks of moving into the house, he arranged for his mother to come live with him. His father had died by this time, and he knew that his mother was lonely and having a difficult time financially. A year later Morgan married Mary Anne Hassek.

An Accidental Discovery

In 1909 Morgan established a second business in Cleveland. He opened a tailor shop that manufactured dresses, coats, and suits with equipment that he had built himself. In a matter of weeks, demand for his clothing was so great that Morgan expanded his operation, and before long the tailor shop had more than 30 employees. His various supervisory and administrative tasks took up a large portion of his day, but he still could not resist tinkering with shop machinery and other devices in hopes of improving his store's productivity.

Within a few months of opening the tailor shop, Morgan became concerned about a problem that the shop was having with woolen fabrics. His workers reported that the high speed of the shop's sewing machines sometimes created too much friction between the sewing needle and the woolen threads. On occasion this friction became so great that it actually scorched the fabric. One night, while working on the problem in a little workshop that he maintained in his home, Morgan dabbed polishing liquid on a sewing needle to see if it would reduce the friction between the needle and the woolen threads. In the

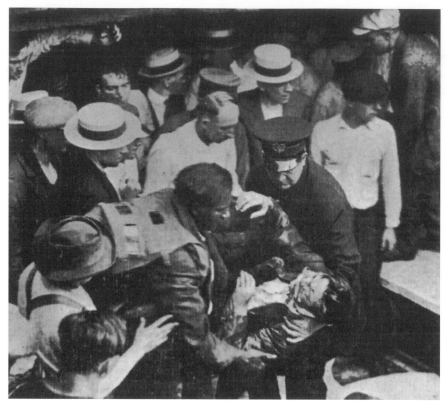

Morgan rescues a worker after the Cleveland Water Works explosion in 1916

middle of his experiment, though, his wife called him for dinner, and he hurriedly wiped the polishing liquid off his hands with a piece of wiry pony fur cloth. When he returned to his workshop after dinner, he was amazed to find that the curly fuzz of the cloth had become straight. Intrigued, he convinced his neighbor, who owned an Airedale terrier, to let him try the liquid on his dog's wiry fur. The solution proved so effective at straightening the dog's hair that the owner barely recognized his pet. Finally, Morgan tried the liquid on his own curly hair, and he was delighted to see that it straightened his hair out as well.

Convinced that he had stumbled upon a potentially popular product, Morgan hurriedly produced large quantities of the liquid. In a matter of months he was marketing the solution as the G.A. Morgan Hair Refining Cream. As he suspected, the solution proved enormously popular with curly haired people who wanted straight hair. By 1913 he had established a company called the G. A. Morgan Refining Company to market the cream; the company remains in operation to this day.

Invention of the Gas Mask

The introduction of Morgan's hair straightening cream added to the entrepreneur's growing reputation as one of Cleveland's brightest businessmen. Lost in the fuss over the hair cream, however, was another Morgan invention that would eventually have a far greater impact on America and the world.

Around the same time that Morgan conducted his hair cream experiments, he also devoted long hours to another project that he was working on. This invention, which he initially called a "breathing device," would enable firefighters, engineers, chemists, and other people to perform hazardous duties without worrying about inhaling dangerous amounts of smoke or harmful gases. On August 19, 1912, Morgan filed a patent application for the device, which also became known as the "Morgan helmet" and the "Morgan safety hood." Morgan described the invention as one that was designed "to provide a portable attachment which will enable a fireman to enter a house filled with thick suffocating gases and smoke and to breathe freely for sometime therein, and thereby enable him to perform his duties of saving life and valuables without danger to himself from suffocation." The device featured a hood that was placed over the user's head and a long tube that extended from an opening in the hood down to the ground. Morgan reasoned that if the tube was long enough, it would enable users to breathe the layer of clean air that can often be found below clouds of smoke and gas. The lower end of the tube was lined with absorbent materials that were moistened with water before use, so that the tube would snag dust and other non-breathable elements before they reached the breathing hood. Morgan also included a separate tube through which users could exhale.

In 1914 Morgan was granted a patent for his gas mask device, and he quickly launched a full-scale effort to sell the product. He established the National Safety Device Company to manufacture the gas masks, and he toured all around the country on behalf of the invention, unveiling a terrific sense of showmanship in the process. But even though he was the inventor of the device, he was careful about publicizing that fact to potential customers. He knew that racism in America was so bad at the time that many white people would not buy his product if they knew its inventor was a black man. In fact, he took on a number of white partners when he created the National Safety Device Company.

Morgan's faith in his gas mask invention was so strong that he made major efforts to convince fellow blacks to invest in the company. He was mostly unsuccessful, however, so few black people reaped the economic benefits when the value of the company's stock surged over subsequent months (it rose from $10 per share in 1914 to more than $250 per share in 1916). Sales of the device were aided significantly when it received a first prize gold medal from the International Exposition for Sanitation and Safety in 1914, but it was not until 1916 that sales really boomed. It was during that year that Morgan used the safety hood in a heroic and highly publicized rescue effort.

On July 24, 1916, a tremendous explosion took place in a tunnel of the Cleveland Waterworks facility. The violent detonation triggered a structural collapse that trapped a number of city workers (published reports place the number of trapped workers at anywhere from 20 to 32) in a section of tunnel that sat more than 250 feet beneath the surface of Lake Erie and more than five miles from shore. Even worse, the explosion flooded the tunnel with smoke and noxious gases that threatened to kill all the trapped workers. Would-be rescuers made several attempts to reach the workers, but they were repeatedly turned back by the clouds of gas and smoke. Finally, though, someone at the scene realized that Morgan's gas mask invention might enable rescuers to brave the horrible mix of thick smoke and gassy fumes.

Roused from sleep in the middle of the night, Morgan immediately enlisted the help of his brother Frank, who helped him carry a number of the hoods to the accident site. Accompanied by his brother and two other volunteers, Morgan charged into the dark tunnel. Protected from the smoke and gas by the masks, the rescuers were able to reach the trapped men. Several of the injured workers were subsequently saved, although published accounts differ significantly in their reports on the total number of men saved. Some sources indicate that anywhere from 20 to 32 workers were saved, while others state that only six men were dragged out of the tunnel, and that only two of them ultimately survived the prolonged exposure to smoke and gas.

But while the total number of men saved may never be known with certainty, no one could dispute the bravery that was shown by the Morgan brothers and the other rescuers. Moreover, everyone recognized that if it had not been for Morgan's gas mask device, all of the workers would have died in the smoke-filled tunnel. To show its appreciation to Morgan, the city of Cleveland awarded him with a gold medal for heroism and publicly hailed him as its "most honored and bravest citizen."

In the wake of the dramatic rescue, fire departments and mining companies from around the country contacted Morgan to place orders for his remarkable device. Unfortunately, though, orders for the hoods tapered off dramatically—especially in the South—when people learned that the masks had been invented by a black man. This saddened Morgan tremendously, for he realized that some firemen and miners around the country would not receive the protection they deserved because of this bigotry.

Morgan's gas mask device was so important, however, that other manufacturers soon flooded the market with their own models, and within a few short years gas masks were standard equipment in many fire halls and mining camps around the country. The invention also was used heavily in the final

Morgan with two of his sons, circa 1920

months of World War I (1914-1918), when Germany turned to poison gas in an unsuccessful attempt to avoid defeat at the hands of the United States and its allies. Historians estimate that the gas mask saved the lives of thousands of soldiers during that conflict.

Invention of the Three-Way Traffic Signal

In the early 1920s Morgan put his creative mind to work on solving a problem that was growing by leaps and bounds in Cleveland and other metropolitan areas. Automobiles had only recently been invented, but the number of cars on the streets was increasing all the time. Collisions between automobiles and horse-drawn carriages were rising at an alarming pace, and car crashes were growing as well. Morgan recognized that many of these terrible collisions were taking place at intersections, where traffic from one street ran into traffic from another street. He knew that a device was needed to control the flow of traffic at such intersections.

On November 20, 1923, after months of hard work, Morgan was awarded a patent for a "traffic signal" that would control the stop-and-go of traffic at intersections. He subsequently sold the rights to this invention to General Electric for $40,000, which was a huge amount of money at that time. Like other traffic signals before it, this invention was manually operated and had arms that swung out with the words "go" and "stop" printed on them. But unlike other models, Morgan's traffic signal had an intermediate position that alerted drivers of an impending signal change. In other words, his traffic signal was the first one that incorporated the "caution" signal that is today shown with a yellow light. Morgan's three-way traffic signal became the model for the stoplights that today are used all around the world to help people travel safely on streets, highways, and railways.

Defender of Black Americans

Morgan had always done his best to help fellow black people in his businesses, but during the 1920s he decided that he wanted to do more. In 1920 he founded a newspaper known as the *Cleveland Call* that was dedicated to providing both local and national news of interest to black people. He also continued his longtime involvement with the Cleveland Association of Colored Men, which eventually merged with the National Association for the Advancement of Colored People (NAACP). In 1931 Morgan made an unsuccessful bid for a seat on the Cleveland City Council. He ran on a platform that emphasized equal treatment of all citizens, black or white. As his granddaughter Karen Morgan later recalled, Garrett Morgan "was a plain man . . . proud to be an American, proud of his race."

In 1943 Morgan developed glaucoma, a disease that affects people's eyesight. For the remainder of his life, he was nearly blind, but he did not let the disease stop him from remaining heavily involved in the affairs of his adopted city. He continued as an active member of the NAACP, and he organized a fraternity of black students at Cleveland's Western Reserve University. Morgan died in Cleveland on July 27, 1963.

MARRIAGE AND FAMILY

Morgan married Mary Anne Hassek in 1908. Their marriage lasted for over 50 years, until his death in 1963. They had three sons—John Pierpont, Garrett Jr., and Cosmo Henry.

HOBBIES AND OTHER INTERESTS

Although Morgan spent a great deal of his free time tinkering with new inventions and working on behalf of other black people, he was also very fond of the outdoors. His granddaughter characterized him as "a lover of the great outdoors, of nature itself."

HONORS AND AWARDS

First Prize Gold Medal (Second International Exposition of Sanitation and
    Safety): 1914
Medal of Honor (International Association of Fire Engineers): 1916
Medal of Heroism (City of Cleveland): 1916

FURTHER READING

Books

African Americans: Voices of Triumph, 1993
Contemporary Black Biography, Vol. 1, 1992
Grolier Library of North American Biographies: Entrepreneurs and Inventors,
    Vol. 3, 1994
Haber, Louis. *Black Pioneers of Science and Invention,* 1970 (juvenile)
Haskins, Jim. *Black Inventors and Their Inventions,* 1991 (juvenile)
Hayden, Robert C. *Nine African-American Inventors,* 1992 (juvenile)
McKissack, Patricia, and Fredrick McKissack. *African-American Inventors,*
    1994 (juvenile)
Notable Twentieth-Century Scientists, 1995
Ploski, Harry A., and James Williams, eds. *The Negro Almanac: A Reference
    Work on the African American,* 1989
Ryan, Elizabeth. *The Biographical Dictionary of Black Americans,* 1992 (juvenile)
Sammons, Vivian O. *Blacks in Science and Medicine,* 1990
Turner, Glennette Tilley. *Take a Walk in Their Shoes,* 1989 (juvenile)
World Book Encyclopedia, 1997

Periodicals

Akron Beacon Journal, Mar. 3, 1997, p.B3
Detroit News, Feb. 5, 1991, p.A1
Encore, Mar. 1974, p.6
Journal of Negro History, Winter/Spring 1985, p.1
School Shop/Tech Directions, Apr. 1992, p.54

Bill Nye 1955-

American Television Personality and Engineer
Host of the Children's Science Show *Bill Nye the Science Guy*

BIRTH

Bill Nye was born November 27, 1955, in Washington, D.C. His parents are Edwin Nye, a retired appliance salesman, and Jacquie Jenkins-Nye, who has a Ph.D. in education. He has one brother and one sister.

YOUTH

"I was turned on to science very young," recalls Nye. "I have clear memories of doing water table experiments in second grade, then mathematics really grabbed me. My older brother took a physics class, and I was just fascinated with the stuff. I can't remember when I *wasn't* interested in science."

Of course, Nye was also interested in a wide range of other activities as a youngster. He loved to play army and spaceship with his friends, and he spent hours playing Frisbee and various sports around the neighborhood in Washington, D.C., where he grew up. But even though those activities were fun, young Nye's fascination with the world around him always led him to spend a lot of time reading and conducting early experiments, too. Even when he was a boy, his parents thought that his curiosity might lead him into a career as a scientist of some sort, and they encouraged him to make the most of his abilities and educational opportunities.

> *"I was turned on to science very young. I have clear memories of doing water table experiments in second grade, then mathematics really grabbed me. My older brother took a physics class, and I was just fascinated with the stuff. I can't remember when I wasn't interested in science."*

EDUCATION

Nye attended school at the private Sidwell Friends School in Washington, D.C. (the same school that "First Daughter" Chelsea Clinton attended years later). Although he now characterizes himself as a "big-time nerd" as a kid, his classmates paint a somewhat different picture. "We had enough oddballs in that school so that there weren't oddballs," recalled one classmate. "Lots of people were physics majors and chess players, carried brief cases and wore short pants, so they didn't stand out. Bill was really gregarious, outspoken, and always making fun of something."

Nye's teachers, meanwhile, describe him as a bright student whose intense curiosity about various subjects made him a pleasure to have in the classroom. "He was excellent in physics," remembered one teacher. "He liked to build things, liked to do things, liked to talk about physics a lot." The teenager's enthusiasm for science was so great, in fact, that he posed for his senior picture with an oscilloscope, a device that produces a visual image of electrical signals. His high energy level also led him to join a variety of school clubs, from the Mad Scientists' Club to the Yo-Yo Team.

For his part, Nye has a lot of fond memories of his elementary and high school years, and he continually tells current students to make the most of their opportunities during that part of their lives. "Stay in school," he stated.

Bill Nye visiting a Montana dinosaur dig with paleontologist Becca Laws

"Your education is priceless. Once you have it, no one can take it away from you. If you learn about the world and science, you'll always have a job doing something you like. Science rules." Nye graduated from Sidwell in 1973.

Nye enrolled at Cornell University, where he took an introductory-level course in astronomy taught by famed scientist Carl Sagan. "Professor Sagan changed my life," Nye later said. "I met him a few times over the years after I took his astronomy course. Each meeting left me refreshed with a new and more intimate understanding of what we had discussed. It came from his easy, deep, and passionate grasp of things. I was always a little awed after each exchange." Nye graduated from Cornell with a bachelor's degree in mechanical engineering in the late 1970s.

CHOOSING A CAREER

After graduating, Nye moved to the Pacific Northwest and worked at various engineering and design firms in the Seattle area from the late 1970s to 1986. He first joined the Boeing plane manufacturing company as an engineer, designing rudder systems for their 747 planes. After three years at Boeing, he quit and took a job at a shipyard making oil-slick skimming boats. He later held jobs in which he designed oil field equipment, a laser gyroscope for airplanes, and a coffee spill-proof volume knob for radios. During non-working hours, meanwhile, Nye tutored inner-city kids and volunteered as a Big Brother.

At the same time, Nye was becoming increasingly involved in Seattle's comedy scene. Soon after arriving in Seattle, he had entered a local Steve Martin look-alike contest and walked off with first prize by dazzling the judges with his wild impressions of the comedian. Encouraged by his success, the outgoing engineer started doing stand-up comedy in the area. By 1986 Nye had decided to devote all his energy to comedy, so he quit his engineering job and joined the cast of a local television comedy show called "Almost Live." Some of his jokes baffled his fellow comedians — one cast member called them "jokes of the future" — but a lot of the people on the show seemed to realize that he was a talented fellow. "Bill always had this frenetic personality — he'd blurt out anything that he was thinking of," remembered a fellow cast member. "He's like a roman candle rolling around on the table spraying things in all directions. If you can just pick it up and focus it in one direction, you've got a hit."

Within months of joining the show, Nye came up with the idea that would eventually splash his face on the television screens of households across America. Inspired by a funny radio bit in which he concluded a summary of his scientific knowledge by referring to himself as "Bill Nye, the Science Guy," he decided to create a character that would enable him to combine his love of science with his comedy material. In 1987 he unveiled the character on "Almost Live." Wearing his own lab coat and safety glasses, Nye dunked an onion in liquid nitrogen and shattered it. The studio audience loved the performance, and Nye immediately realized that he was on to something. "It hit me so hard," he remembered. "Here was everything I wanted to do. With science, and being funny, all at once." In a matter of weeks, Bill Nye the Science Guy was one of the most popular characters on the show. Nye had great fun coming up with entertaining demonstrations of scientific principles. "I perfected a trick — this is *my* special trick! — of eating a frozen marshmallow so steam comes out your nose!" he recalled.

CAREER HIGHLIGHTS

Nye was convinced that the Science Guy would be a great host for an entertaining show about science. After enlisting the help of local producers Jim McKenna and Erren Gottlieb, Nye started pitching the idea to the Public

Broadcasting System (PBS), MTV, the major networks, and other television avenues. But for four years he had no luck in selling his idea. "It was a difficult time because I made no money and lived in an apartment so small that I had to hang my bicycle from the ceiling to save space," Nye remembered. "My engineer friends were buying houses with hot tubs in the suburbs and acquiring new wives. I was over 30 and had no future. Then I got lucky with several educational videos for the Washington State Department of Ecology."

Nye's performances on the educational videos and "Almost Live" kept his character fresh, and in 1993 his persistence finally paid off. Early that year, he received a call from Elizabeth Brock, an executive with KCTS, Seattle's public television station. Brock thought that Nye's Science Guy character would be an ideal host for a children's show about science. She asked him if he would be interested in producing a sample show (known as a "pilot") to see if the concept would work. Nye was delighted with the offer, and in April 1993 the pilot episode aired nationally on PBS.

Nye was excited about the pilot, but he had experienced so many disappointments over the previous few years that he did not want to get his hopes up. In fact, shortly after wrapping up the pilot episode he decided to go on a long vacation. "That weekend I went out and bought a brand new sleeping bag," Nye remembered. "I said, 'This is it — I'm gonna ride my bike across the country.'"

Before Nye could leave, however, he learned that Buena Vista Television, a subsidiary of the Walt Disney Co., was interested in his show. Disney was looking for shows that would meet the requirements of the 1990 Children's Television Act. This law called for local television stations to broadcast a specific numbers of hours per week of educational shows for children. The company subsequently reached an agreement with KCTS in which *Bill Nye the Science Guy* would be broadcast on both public and commercial television stations. KCTS would take care of production, and Buena Vista would handle distribution. Both KCTS and Disney agreed to invest money in the show, and the National Science Federation chipped in with a generous contribution as well. Suddenly, after years of frustration, Nye's dreams of hosting an entertaining show about science were about to come true.

Debut of a Hit Show

Bill Nye the Science Guy was unveiled in the fall of 1993. It was an immediate favorite with kids, and with many adults, too. After only an episode or two, viewers across the nation realized that the show and its host were true originals. The show, which was the first series ever shown simultaneously on commercial TV and PBS, offered a terrific blend of humor, special effects, music videos, colorful graphics, and basic science. As *Mediaweek* observed, Nye's show "offers an intense half-hour of wacky science instruction designed not only to teach but to leave kids with the perception that science is 'cool.'"

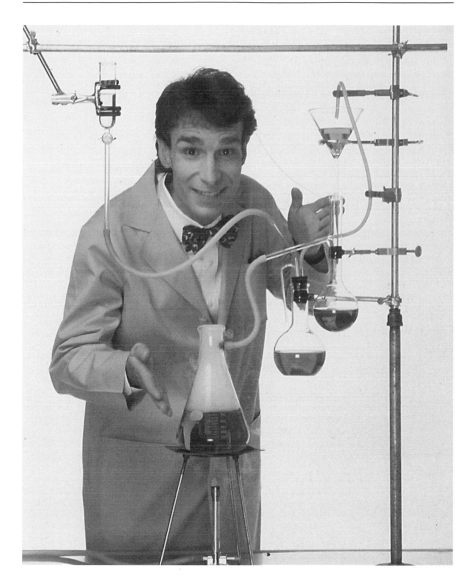

Television critics and kids alike agreed that the key to the show's success was its madcap host. According to one public television executive, "He's geeky but cool at the same time. He gives nerds a better chance in life because he's hip." Wearing a lab coat and bow tie, Nye seems willing to do just about anything to inform viewers about scientific principles, as *Newsweek* explains here. "[Nye] spouts steam from his nose. He pounds nails with a frozen banana. He waves his arms and yells a lot, dons outrageous hats, plunges down waters slides, even spritzes the camera. All to prove that science can be fun, or, as Nye himself describes it: '*Waaay* cool!'" Nye often ventured outside of the

131

studio to help young viewers gain a greater understanding and appreciation of science, too. In the first few seasons of the show, for example, he barrel-rolled in a stunt plane to demonstrate principles of flight, parasailed over Puget Sound to explain principles of velocity and lift, and helicoptered into the crater of Mount St. Helens to talk about the earth's crust.

But as Nye explained, all of the show's fast-paced activity is ultimately aimed at educating children about science. "It looks like a frantic madhouse, but there's a deep, deep plan behind the show," he said. Television critics and children's advocates agreed. They noted that each episode of *Bill Nye the Science Guy* is focused to help viewers remember one or two important points. Observers also pointed out that the show features kids demonstrating experiments that can be done safely at home. In addition, Nye tries to encourage girls and minority children to learn about science by making sure that children and other scientists that appear on the show include women and nonwhites. "Girls and kids of color are traditionally excluded from science, discouraged from pursuing a career in science," Nye said.

Scientists praised the show, too. They noted that Nye's character is a likable one, whereas many other scientists on television are portrayed as coldhearted or evil. Even more importantly, they applauded the show's decision not to broadcast misleading or inaccurate information for the sake of entertainment. "In one episode," recounted the *Seattle Times*, "a hammer fell on the moon and some audio engineer made it go CLUNK. Upon hearing this, Nye stopped joking and turned granite-like. The moon has no atmosphere, the Science Guy pointed out. Ergo, the hammer couldn't make a noise." In order to ensure that each episode of *Bill Nye the Science Guy* is accurate in every way, a panel of scientific advisors reviews all finished scripts.

Within two years of the show's debut, various *Bill Nye the Science Guy* materials had become hugely popular with kids and teachers alike. "Science Guy" books, videos, teaching guides, software programs, and student science kits popped up everywhere, as growing numbers of teachers embraced Nye's zany way of teaching about science. "The show is used extensively by tens of thousands of teachers," said Nye. "And that's so gratifying. It amazes me. It thrills me. I'll get pictures of teachers dressed like me and letters saying, 'My kids want me to be like you.' And I say, 'Go for it,' because when you're teaching, you have to be entertaining. You have to hold their attention. That is your job."

More than four years after *Bill Nye the Science Guy* first hit the airwaves, the show remains one of the most popular children's shows in the country. Once in a while, Nye still seems stunned by the ways in which his life has changed because of that success. "Getting the show," he said, "was the strangest thing that's ever happened to me." He also realizes how fortunate he is to be doing something that he loves. "My whole life has been a preparation for this show," he added. "The show is an extension of me."

Bill Nye the science guy and 11-year-old Cass Thompson panning for minerals, fossils, dinosaur bones, ancient sea turtles, and petrified wood

Sparking an Interest in Science

For Nye, in fact, teaching children about science has become his mission. "You know, my little goal on the show is to change the world," Nye said. "I am a happy-go-lucky guy, but give me a world problem—hole in the ozone, people infected with HIV, Somalia—for me, the solution is fundamentally a science solution. The people who are going to solve these problems are not people my age. . . . It will be people much, much younger." He also hopes that his show will help reverse a general downward trend in people's interest in science. "[You] can't run around taking it all for granted, I'm telling you. That will be our undoing as a society, if we keep this stuff up. Because you can't have [science] understood by just a few, an elite. That's a formula for disaster. Suppose they decide to quit coming to work, or suppose they make a big mistake? What I'm trying to do is to get young people excited about science, so in the future we'll have more scientists."

Nye plans to continue hosting *Bill Nye the Science Guy* for years to come, but he also hopes to branch out into other projects in the future. In 1997, for example, Nye was asked to narrate a new documentary called *Astronauts*. This documentary will profile a year in the life of the six astronauts chosen for the Endeavor crew of Space Shuttle Flight STS-72. "I'd love to do more narrating," he said. "It's cool. It's very exciting. But also, it's the direction that I want to take my career. It's more serious. I also like to talk about the thing that I'm so passionate about, which is science."

Nye is also excited about the project because he has always been fascinated by space exploration. In fact, Nye has applied to join America's astronaut program, although he admits his chances of gaining admittance are pretty slim. He thinks that space travel is on the brink of an exciting era of discovery. "Flying in space is very dangerous," he admitted. "Take-off is a few people sitting on top of 100 tons of explosive. But we learn about the planet by going into space. We learn about the Earth, our home, by going into space. . . . We may live at the time when life is discovered on another body in our solar system. Or how about this? We'll live at a time when we know for sure—or we're pretty sure—that there isn't life on other bodies in the solar system, and that's pretty interesting, too. Don't you want to go find out? Whatever it is? Don't you want to know?"

HOME AND FAMILY

Nye lives in a two-bedroom house that overlooks Seattle's Elliott Bay. He has never been married, and he admits that his hectic schedule makes it hard for him to establish a relationship with anyone. "He is the first person here in the morning and the last person to leave," confirmed one of the show's staff members. "Unless he is sleeping, Bill Nye is working."

MAJOR INFLUENCES

When asked about those who have influenced him, Nye mentions such diverse figures as TV science personality Mr. Wizard, comedian Steve Martin, and astronomer Carl Sagan.

HOBBIES AND OTHER INTERESTS

Nye has a lot of different hobbies, although he sometimes complains that he doesn't have enough time to enjoy them these days. In addition to bicycling, hiking, ultimate Frisbee, swimming, and jogging, he likes to scuba dive in Hawaii, play with Lionel trains, shoot off model rockets, and dance. "Ballroom dancing is a fabulously good way to get exercise," he said. "Country western [dancing] is the same thing." Finally, Nye says that he enjoys "making things." He notes that he recently patented a round magnifying glass made out of a plastic bag filled with water.

CREDITS

Bill Nye the Science Guy, 1993 — (TV series)

WRITINGS

Bill Nye the Science Guy's Big Blast of Science, 1993
Bill Nye the Science Guy's Please Consider the Following—A Way Cool Set of Science Questions, Answers and Ideas to Ponder, 1995

HONORS AND AWARDS

Parents' Choice Award: 1993, 1994, 1995, for *Bill Nye the Science Guy*
International Monitor Award: 1995, for Best Achievement in Children's Programming
Silver Apple Award: 1996 (2 awards), for *Bill Nye the Science Guy*
Daytime Emmy Awards: 1996 (two awards); 1997 (four awards), for *Bill Nye the Science Guy*
Science Society of Presidents Award: 1997

FURTHER READING

Baltimore Sun, Aug. 7, 1995, p.D1
Boys' Life, Apr. 1995, p.5
Child's Life, Sep. 1995, p.24
Christian Science Monitor, Feb. 2, 1995, p.12
Family PC Magazine, July/Aug. 1995, p.159
Los Angeles Times, Mar. 5, 1997, p.E2
Mediaweek, May 16, 1994, p.14
New York Times, Apr. 9, 1997, p.B1
Newsweek, Sep. 20, 1993, p.54
People, Oct. 21, 1996, p.69
Popular Science, May 1997, p.31
Seattle Post-Intelligencer, Aug. 6, 1996, p.D1
Seattle Times, Sep. 24, 1989, p.J1; Dec. 18, 1994, p.12

ADDRESS

Buena Vista Television
500 South Buena Vista Street
Burbank, CA 91521

WORLD WIDE WEB SITE

http://nyelabs.kcts.org

Eloy Rodriguez 1947-

American Plant Chemist and Biologist
Founder of the Field of Zoopharmacognosy

BIRTH

Eloy Rodriguez was born on January 7, 1947, in Edinburg, Texas, a mostly Hispanic community in the southern tip of the state, near both the Mexican border and the Gulf of Mexico. His father, Everardo Rodriguez, immigrated to the United States from Mexico as a migrant worker and later became a short-order cook. His mother, Hilaria (Calvillo) Rodriguez, worked cleaning other people's houses.

YOUTH

Rodriguez grew up in a poor neighborhood, in a small frame house perched on stilts. "We were so poor that crime really didn't pay. I mean, who do you steal from in a neighborhood like ours?" he once remarked. "If you stole a car, you probably got into greater debt trying to fix the darn thing!" Throughout his childhood, he enjoyed spending time with his large extended family. Several aunts and uncles—as well as a total of 67 cousins—lived within a few blocks of his house. Rodriguez began working at an early age to help his family make ends meet. He was a migrant worker. He traveled with other family members to nearby farms and helped pick cotton, strawberries, and cherries. "I *hated* it," he recalled. "I swore I'd never do it again. It's why you got an education."

Despite his poverty, Rodriguez had a variety of experiences as a boy that helped prepare him for his later career as a scientist studying the chemicals produced by plants. "My interest in science started with visits to my grandfather in Mexico. He had a ranch, a small farm actually. He would always take me out and show me animals and plants. I was intrigued with them, and I think it just stayed with me," he explained. "Certainly my study of medicinal plants has to do with my Chicano and Native American roots also. The only kind of medication that we used to get, I remember very clearly, was people bringing in herbs (primarily women did this). My aunt always maintained a little medicinal garden in the backyard. . . . The more I think about it now, the more I realize the value of those herbal treatments. I know now that the reason these plants work is because they have certain chemicals in them."

EDUCATION

Most members of the older generation in Rodriguez's family were uneducated. His father quit school after the first grade, and his mother only lasted through the seventh. But they "all knew that education was really important," he stated. "Education would be the way out. And all of us, the kids, we could see that." Rodriguez credits his mother, in particular, for encouraging him to do well in school. She dragged him out of bed every morning and always celebrated his academic achievements. Since the family could not afford to buy books, she brought home copies of *Reader's Digest* and old encyclopedia volumes from the wealthy people whose homes she cleaned.

Even though Rodriguez was very intelligent, school was not always enjoyable for him. When he was in elementary school, in the mid-1950s, public schools in Texas would not allow Hispanic students to speak Spanish. In fact, Rodriguez was often punished for speaking the language he used at home. "They hit me on my hands and made me write on the blackboard, 'I will not speak Spanish,'" he recalled. "They had this idea that your brain didn't have the capacity to handle two languages." His non-Hispanic classmates teased him because he brought burritos and tacos for lunch, so Rodriguez begged his mother to make him peanut-butter-and-jelly sandwiches instead.

Despite such problems, Rodriguez was an excellent student. In fact, he never missed a day of school between first grade and twelfth grade. He took college-preparatory classes in high school and graduated in the top five percent of his class. Amazingly, his high school guidance counselor still discouraged him from going on to college, suggesting instead that he enroll in a vocational school and become a mechanic. Rodriguez attributed the counselor's advice to racial stereotypes of Hispanics as laborers. Fortunately, Rodriguez ignored this advice. "I told [the counselor], 'But I don't even know where the engine is in a car.' And I really didn't. I couldn't have cared less about that stuff," he stated.

Studying to Become a Scientist

After graduating from high school in 1965, Rodriguez went to Pan-American University in Edinburg, where he originally planned to major in accounting. "I was going to be a CPA," he explained. "I'd never really thought about being a scientist. It wasn't something many Hispanics seemed to do. I always say I saw my first snowflake before I saw my first Hispanic scientist." But after taking a few science classes, Rodriguez became interested in biology and transferred to the University of Texas at Austin to pursue a zoology degree. At first, his college experience was not very fulfilling. "As an undergraduate I felt very lonely," he noted. "I was one of a very small number of minority students. There were no programs for minority students. We were kind of abandoned. It was like shopping at a 7-11 store—just get your stuff and get out. That was my experience until I got hooked on research!"

> *In school, Rodriguez was often punished for speaking his native Spanish. "They hit me on my hands and made me write on the blackboard, 'I will not speak Spanish.' They had this idea that your brain didn't have the capacity to handle two languages."*

The turning point for Rodriguez came when he got a work-study job as a janitor cleaning the lab of Tom Mabry, a plant biochemist. At first Rodriguez was not allowed to do any lab work, but he watched the experiments that Mabry and his students conducted with great interest. Eventually, some of Mabry's assistants started training Rodriguez to use the lab equipment to extract and isolate chemicals in plants. He turned out to be very good at it, and before long he was running the lab. "The research bug got to me, the passion, the excitement of science," he explained. "Once it gets you, you can't let go of it."

Rodriguez earned his bachelor's degree in 1969 in zoology, and then continued on at the University of Texas to earn his doctorate, or Ph.D., in 1975 in plant biology and phytochemistry (the study of chemicals produced by plants). After completing his doctorate, he did a year of postdoctoral study at the University of British Columbia in Vancouver, Canada. By this time, he had published 20 scientific papers in professional journals about the results of his research. Impressively, his achievements were matched by many of the younger members of his extended family: of the 67 cousins that lived nearby when Rodriguez was growing up, 64 of them graduated from college, and 10 went on to earn graduate degrees.

CAREER HIGHLIGHTS

Studying the Chemicals Produced by Plants

After completing his education, Rodriguez was hired as an assistant professor of toxicology and environmental medicine at the University of California at Irvine (UC Irvine) in 1976. He became the first American-born Latino to teach science at the school. "All along, I was very aware that I was the first this, the first that, and I knew, I *knew* these guys were waiting for me to slip up," he said. Instead, Rodriguez worked hard at both his teaching and his research. He even moved a cot into his lab so that he could work 18 hours per day. Although he did not enjoy much of a social life during this time, his hard work paid off when he was promoted to associate professor in 1978 and full professor in 1983.

Rodriguez's early research focused on the study of plant chemistry, known as phytochemistry. All plants manufacture a variety of chemicals, the best known of which is chlorophyll, which helps plants convert sunlight into energy and also gives them their green color. Specific parts of plants produce different types of chemicals to serve different purposes. For example, flowers produce nice fragrances and colors in order to attract insects and birds to pollinate them. Leaves produce a variety of alkaloid compounds, some of which are designed to make a plant taste bad to animals and insects. Likewise, roots often produce chemicals that repel the fungi and parasitic worms found in soil.

Some plant species — especially those found in the tropical rain forests near the Earth's equator — produce toxic chemicals to help protect themselves against enemies. "There is a large array of organisms that eat plants, and a plant can't just get up and run," Rodriguez explained. "A plant's ability to survive is really due to chemistry — the ability to have an effect on the physiology of an organism. An animal will eat a plant and then either become paralyzed or otherwise impaired by the secondary compounds, or it will escape and learn to avoid that plant in the future."

Some of Rodriguez's earliest research and scientific papers covered the chemical compounds produced by *Parthenium hysterophorus,* a plant from the Compositae family (which also includes sunflowers and daisies) that grew near his college apartment in Texas. He was aware that the same plant grew in Mexico, and that the Mexican version looked very different. These differences intrigued Rodriguez and led him to conduct an extended study of the plant's chemistry. Over time, he became known as an expert on plants in the Compositae family.

Discovering That Animals Use Plant Chemicals as Medicine

In 1984, Rodriguez got a call from Richard Wrangham, a primatologist (a scientist who studies primates) from Harvard University. Wrangham had noticed that the chimpanzees he was studying in East Africa would eat the leaves of the Aspilia plant, another member of the Compositae family, whenever they appeared to be feeling ill. "Apes get every illness that humans get," Rodriguez noted. "You can tell when they are sick; they are lethargic and stay in their tree nests." Wrangham was amazed to observe that the ill chimpanzees would carefully select young Aspilia leaves and swallow them whole, and before long their symptoms would improve. He formed a hypothesis that the chimpanzees were intentionally eating the leaves as medicine rather than as food. Then he asked Rodriguez to find out whether the Aspilia leaves had chemical properties that would support his theory.

"Richard told me he'd seen these sick chimpanzees swallowing Aspilia leaves whole," Rodriguez recalled. "But these are very bitter plants, and so they were making faces like they were tasting something as nasty as cod-liver oil. And as soon as I heard that, I said: 'This is exciting. Get me that plant and get it to me right away.'" Rodriguez analyzed samples of the leaves and found that they contained a chemical called thiarubrine-A, which was toxic to certain fungi and viruses. So the chimpanzees could have been eating the leaves as medicine in order to get rid of viruses or internal parasites, like hookworms. More study would be necessary to prove that the chimpanzees used plant chemicals as medicine intentionally, but it was a very promising development. In 1989, Rodriguez and Wrangham turned their discovery into a new field of scientific study called zoopharmacognosy, which Rodriguez described as "the study of how animals medicate themselves with plants."

As soon as Rodriguez and Wrangham reported the results of their research in scientific journals, animal behaviorists from all over the world began reporting other observations of animals using plant materials in their surroundings as medicine. For example, Kodiak bears were often seen rubbing certain types of roots on their fur, apparently because they contained chemicals that repelled insects. "The response we got was incredible, from both scientists and non-scientists. It's like everyone who owns a dog or cat was telling you that they should be part of this discovery," Rodriguez noted. "This kind of science really catches the imagination of everybody. It's kind of interesting how this field has really exploded in the sense that a lot of scientists from other disciplines are asking questions related to self-medication in animals."

Using Plant Chemicals to Treat Human Illnesses

These discoveries have promising implications for humans, as well. Rodriguez hopes that by studying the way that animals use the chemicals in plants as medicine, he can isolate and synthesize some of these chemicals and use them to treat human illnesses. A wide variety of useful medications have been derived from plant sources. For example, aspirin came from white willow tree bark, the painkillers morphine and codeine came from poppy flowers, the chemotherapy drugs vincristine and vinblastine came from rosy periwinkle leaves, the heart medication digitalis came from the foxglove plant, and the malaria treatment quinine came from cinchona tree bark. Thiarubrine-A, the chemical that Rodriguez found in Aspilia leaves, is now used as an antibiotic and is being tested as a treatment for cancer and Acquired Immune Deficiency Syndrome (AIDS). Other plant-based chemicals are used to protect food crops from insects or to improve the health of domestic animals.

There are many more new chemicals waiting to be discovered in the enormous variety of plant life that exists on Earth. The problem for scientists is figuring out how to focus the search for useful chemicals. Rodriguez believes that animals, as well as traditional healers from native cultures, can provide scientists with valuable clues about which plants to examine first. "A result of this new field [zoopharmacognosy] is that there is now a more direct way to go after plant parts to look at the chemistry. A lot of collection is done randomly—you go out and collect a mixture of leaves, both young and mature. It is a very tedious and not exactly a very rational way to go about getting drugs. It is nice when you have animals basically telling you, 'Here, try these leaves,'" he explained. "Some people might say, 'Well, these are just quirky, anecdotal things that animals and people do.' But for me, it means we should pay attention. If these animals are doing something weird with a plant, you can bet there's a chemical involved. And then it becomes an obsession. I *have* to get that plant."

So far, the tropical rain forests have proven to be the best source of plant chemicals with medical uses. In fact, substances derived from tropical plants can be found in more than 25 percent of all advanced medicines, and in 70 percent of anti-cancer drugs. Still, less than one percent of all rain forest plants have been tested by scientists. "The rain forest contains the most toxic plants and animals and the worst infectious diseases on Earth," Rodriguez stated. "The plant world has evolved many natural chemicals for defense. We've only just scratched the surface." Rodriguez feels that the vast number of valuable compounds yet to be found makes preserving the rain forests particularly important. Yet 50 million acres of rain forest disappear each year—an area the size of the state of Washington—as the world's population grows and that land is cleared to raise crops or graze cattle. "There is no question that diversity, any kind of diversity, is worth keeping. In the tropical rain forest we are talking about the ultimate diversity in plants, animals, fungi—life!" Rodriguez noted. "But the importance of the rain forest goes beyond human concerns. I think we are talking about the health of the planet."

Rodriguez has traveled all over the world conducting research and searching for promising new plant chemicals. His work has taken him from the deserts of the United States and China to the jungles of Africa and South America. During his travels, he has come close to being eaten by a crocodile, and he has been charged by an irritated silver-back gorilla. Nonetheless, Rodriguez enjoys combining field observation with laboratory analysis and thus gaining a broader view of science. "As an undergraduate, I started as a zoology major, then I went into botany, and then organic chemistry. But I never really could separate them. They always work together, and one discipline reinforces the others," he explained. "Never in a lifetime would I have stumbled across the idea of zoopharmacognosy if I had just been stuck within an isolated field of organic chemistry."

Serving as a Role Model for Hispanic Students

In addition to conducting field research and lab work, another aspect of Rodriguez's job as a professor at UC Irvine involved sharing his love of science with students. He particularly enjoyed serving as a role model for young Hispanic students who might not otherwise think of studying science. Because of his own background, he knew how difficult it could be for these students to go to college and make science a career. To address this situation, Rodriguez set up five highly regarded science programs for minority students ranging in age from kindergarten to graduate school. His programs helped double the number of Hispanic students majoring in the sciences at UC Irvine. "I think what really got to me, being a successful professor and a minority scientist, was constantly being told that the school drop-out rate for the Chicano/Latino community was around 60 percent," he recalled. "I thought, my God, that is unbelievable—no society should allow that to happen! We are always concerned about crime, but it all feeds off an uneducated community. I thought that this was one that I could tackle as an educator."

One popular program Rodriguez established was Kids Investigating and Discovering Science (KIDS). Each summer, he brought minority children from poor local families into his lab at UC Irvine, outfitted them in small white lab coats, and gave them hands-on experiences with science. The intensive, month-long program soon grew to include a number of other bilingual science teachers from minority backgrounds. "Most of the kids have never met a scientist. They know nothing about what they do, or why you would want to

> *"I think what really got to me, being a successful professor and a minority scientist, was constantly being told that the school drop-out rate for the Chicano/Latino community was around 60 percent. I thought, my God, that is unbelievable—no society should allow that to happen! We are always concerned about crime, but it all feeds off an uneducated community. I thought that this was one that I could tackle as an educator."*

be one," he explained. "When you have minorities in the classroom at many schools around here, these are kids who are generally not called upon by the teacher to answer questions. There is some stereotyping about them. We believe that with time and attention paid to kids, they will do well. Some of the parents came up to me . . . and wanted to know what we were doing to their kids, because on the weekends their kids were actually asking, 'When are we going to go back to school?'"

Rodriguez also helped establish the California Alliance for Minority Participation in the Sciences (CAMP) program, which is designed to attract more minorities to the study of science. CAMP provides tutoring, guidance, and special summer programs to students from grade school through college. The program received $5 million in funding from the National Science Foundation in 1991. "This is seed money for these students," Rodriguez noted. "It is a way for them to discover that science is great and wonderful and that they can indeed find a future in it." The success of these and other programs earned Rodriguez several awards.

In 1995, Rodriguez left UC Irvine to take a new job as the James A. Perkins Chair of Environmental Studies at Cornell University in Ithaca, New York. He thus became the first American-born Latino to hold an endowed position in the sciences. At Cornell, he has a lab in a state-of-the-art biotechnology complex, and before long he will be able to grow his own plants in a simulated tropical rain forest. "My coming to Cornell is like coming to paradise in terms of my scientific research," he noted.

MARRIAGE AND FAMILY

Rodriguez married Helena Viramontes on June 5, 1982. The couple met at UC Irvine when he was an associate professor and she was a graduate student. Viramontes, who is now a well-known writer and Hispanic activist, had won a national literary contest and was invited to read her story at an awards ceremony. Rodriguez, who attended the ceremony, gave her a standing ovation afterward. "She was attractive and smart, and I thought to myself, 'That's a nice combination,'" he recalled. "She was extremely shy and surrounded by her family, and it was like getting through a circle of covered wagons." After they married, Rodriguez cut back his working hours at the lab from 18 to 14 per day. They eventually had two children, daughter Pilar and son Eloy Francisco. Rodriguez and his family now live near Cornell University in Ithaca, New York.

WRITINGS

Biology and Chemistry of Plant Trichomes, 1984

HONORS AND AWARDS

Research Career Development Award (National Institute of Allergy and
    Infectious Diseases): 1982-87
First Hispanic Educator Award (League of United Latin American Citizens):
    1984
Professional Research Accomplishment Recognition (*Los Angeles Times*): 1989
Outstanding Professor (*Hispanic Business*): 1991
Martin de la Cruz Medallion (Mexican Academy of Traditional Medicine): 1992

FURTHER READING

Books

American Men and Women of Science, 1994
Who's Who among Spanish Americans, 1994-95
Who's Who in America, 1994

Periodicals

American Biology Teacher, May 1996, p.282
Chronicle of Higher Education, July 7, 1995, p.A5
Fort Lauderdale Sun-Sentinel, Oct. 4, 1992, p.E1
Hispanic, Sep. 1996, p.36
Los Angeles Times, Oct. 17, 1989, p.A1; Aug. 5, 1990, p.B1; Sep. 9, 1990, p.B3;
    May 15, 1991, p.B3; Dec. 12, 1991, p.A3
National Wildlife, Dec. 1993-Jan. 1994, p.46
New York Times Biographical Service, Dec. 1994, p.1956
New York Times Magazine, Dec. 18, 1994, p.50
Sacramento Bee, Feb. 8, 1992, p.A1
Science, Nov. 13, 1992, p.1190
Washington Post, Feb. 17, 1991, p.C3

ADDRESS

Cornell University
Department of Environmental Studies
Ithaca, NY 14850

An Wang 1920-1990

Chinese-Born American Physicist, Inventor, and
Businessman
Founder of Wang Laboratories

BIRTH

An Wang, whose name means "Peaceful King," was born in
Shanghai, China, on February 7, 1920. He was the second of five
children born to Yin Lu Wang, who taught English at an elementary school outside of Shanghai, and Zen Wan (Chien)
Wang, who was a homemaker. An had an older sister, Hsu, a
younger sister, Yu, and two younger brothers, Ping and Ge. After
moving to the United States in 1945, An became a naturalized
American citizen in 1955.

YOUTH

Although Wang was born into a loving, middle-class family, his early years were not without hardship. He grew up during a troubled period of Chinese history known as the "Age of Confusion," when different factions were fighting for control of the government. Wang described this difficult period as "the struggle for the soul of China after centuries of medieval rule." While the country experienced ongoing civil disturbances in the first half of the 20th century, it was also engaged in a long conflict with neighboring Japan, which culminated in Japan's invasion of China just prior to World War II. These events cast a dark shadow over Wang's childhood.

————— " —————

"I am never quite able to convince people that I did not suffer culture shock when I arrived in the United States. People insist that I must have been overwhelmed by the things that make America different from China — the wealth, the people, even the food. But this is simply not true. I look for the similarities between cultures, not the differences."

————— " —————

Still, Wang did enjoy some aspects of his youth. He spent a lot of time reading books at the local library, especially biographies of great scientists like Galileo, Isaac Newton, and the Wright Brothers. He also learned about Chinese literature and Confucian thought from his grandmother. Confucian thought originated with the ancient Chinese philosopher Confucius, who emphasized peace, justice, living a simple life, and serving the community. Wang later said that these values helped him in his business career.

EDUCATION

When Wang was six years old, his family moved to Kun San, about 30 miles north of Shanghai, where his father taught English at a private school. Even though classes at the school started with the third grade, Wang begged his parents to enroll him anyway. He thus entered third grade at age six and remained two years younger than his classmates throughout his years of schooling in China. He soon learned to handle the schoolwork and get along with his fellow students, but he admitted that at first it was like "being thrown in the water when you don't know how to swim. You either learn how to swim — and fast — or you sink!" Wang always found math and science to be very easy, but he sometimes had trouble with geography and history. He also started studying English in fourth grade.

At this time, obtaining an education in China was a very competitive process. The public schools did not have enough room for all the students who wanted to attend, so students had to pass an entrance examination to be admitted.

Since Wang was so young, his father wanted him to wait a year before taking the test to enter junior high. But Wang took the test anyway and got the highest score of any student. "I took those exams on my own, without telling anyone," he recalled. "Then the scores were posted. My score was number one. I came in first. That's when I began to develop real self-confidence." After posting good grades in junior high and scoring well on another test, he was admitted to Shanghai Provincial High School—one of the best schools in China—at age 13. The school required students to live on campus, so Wang had to move away from home at this time. Many of his courses there were taught in English and used the same textbooks that American college students used. Wang graduated from high school in 1936.

Wang entered Chiao Tung University in Shanghai and majored in electrical engineering with a specialty in communications. Because of his excellent test scores and grades, he was named president of his class. His youth and small size prevented him from competing in team sports, but he did join the university's table tennis (Ping Pong) team. He also contributed to a student newspaper, translating articles about science and technology from American magazines like *Popular Mechanics* and *Popular Science* into Chinese. In 1937, during his sophomore year, Japan invaded China. Since the city of Shanghai was a major target for the Japanese, Chiao Tung University was moved into a nearby "international zone" governed by the French. This nine-square-mile area was like an island of calm as war raged all around. Wang graduated from college in 1940.

Wang worked at the university for a year as a teaching assistant in electrical engineering. The following year he decided that he wanted to make a contribution to the war effort. China was an ally of the United States during World War II, fighting against Japan and Germany. He volunteered to go to Kweilin in central China to help design and build radio transmitters for the government troops. His group of engineers was forced into the hills by weekly Japanese bombing raids. They took shelter in caves and passed the time by playing card games until the attacks ended. Still, Wang claimed that he enjoyed the challenge of creating working radios out of substitute materials when parts became unavailable due to wartime shortages. He continued in this position until World War II ended in 1945 and Japan was forced to withdraw from China. Sadly, the war took a terrible toll on his family, as both of his parents and his older sister died during the conflict. Because of his years away at school, the war, and his later move to the United States, Wang did not see his younger siblings for 40 years.

Moving to the United States

Wang soon accepted an opportunity to go to the United States for a two-year apprenticeship program intended to prepare young engineers to help rebuild China. After a long journey by boat, he arrived in America in June 1945. "I am never quite able to convince people that I did not suffer culture shock when I arrived in the United States," he stated. "People insist that I must have been overwhelmed by the things that make America different from China—the wealth, the people, even the food. But this is simply not true. I look for the similarities between cultures, not the differences." His strong command of English made the transition easier for him.

—— " ——

After the Chinese Civil War, Wang decided to remain in the U.S. rather than return to his homeland. "I knew myself well enough to know that I could not thrive under a totalitarian Communist system. I had long been independent, and I wanted to continue to make my own decisions about my life."

—— " ——

After his arrival, Wang decided that he could learn more as a graduate student than he could through the apprenticeship program. He entered Harvard University in September 1945 and earned his master's degree the following year. After working at a clerical job with a Chinese government supply agency in Ottawa, Canada, for a short time, he returned to Harvard and earned his doctorate (Ph.D.) in physics in 1948. By this time, the civil war that had rocked China during Wang's boyhood had resumed. There was widespread fighting between the Nationalist forces led by Chiang Kai-shek and the Communist forces led by Mao Zedong, and it appeared that Mao's forces would gain control of the country. As a result, Wang decided to remain in the United States permanently rather than return to his homeland. "I knew myself well enough to know that I could not thrive under a totalitarian Communist system," he explained. "I had long been independent, and I wanted to continue to make my own decisions about my life."

CAREER HIGHLIGHTS

Designing Memory Cores for Early Computers

During his Ph.D. studies, Wang began working as a research assistant in the Harvard Computation Laboratory. It was there that a team of scientists, led by Dr. Howard Aiken, created one of the first computers ever to operate in the United States. This machine, called the Mark I, filled an entire room and was very noisy, but it still represented a significant breakthrough in computer development. Wang's education was not strictly related to computer science, which was a new field at that time, so it was really a matter of chance that he ended up working in Aiken's lab. "By accident I got an opportunity to help make history," he noted.

One day, in trying to refine and improve the Mark I, Aiken asked Wang for his input on an important problem. The young physicist was "to find a way to record and read magnetically stored information without mechanical motion," Wang recalled. This problem had stumped Aiken and his team for years. But the solution came to Wang in a flash as he was walking through Harvard Yard. Within three weeks, he had invented the "magnetic memory core" — a ground-breaking method of data storage that would be used in computers for the next 20 years.

Wang's breakthrough used tiny, donut-shaped metal storage elements, called cores, that could be magnetized in either a positive or negative direction. Each magnetically charged core stored one binary digit, or bit, of information. The computer could read the direction of the magnetic charges and convert them into binary digits of zero or one. The sequence of zeroes and ones formed a language that the computer could understand and use to perform its computations. The main problem that Wang encountered with this system was that when the computer read the direction of the magnetic charge on the cores, it caused the charge to reverse, thus destroying the information that was stored there. But rather than trying to find a way to prevent the computer from destroying the information, as other scientists had done, Wang simply had the computer restore the data after using it. "It did not matter whether or not I destroyed the information while reading it," he realized. "I could simply *rewrite* the data immediately afterward. Moreover, since magnetic flux could be changed in a few thousandths of a second, I could do this without any real sacrifice of speed." Wang's memory cores formed the basis of computer data storage technology until they were replaced by the silicon microchips that are used today.

Founding Wang Laboratories

By the early 1950s, Harvard was reducing its emphasis on computer research. Even though he only had $600 in savings, Wang decided to patent his memory core invention and start his own company, Wang Laboratories. When it opened for business in June 1951, Wang Laboratories consisted of a small, unfurnished office in Boston and only one employee — Wang himself. Many of his Chinese friends thought that he was making a mistake, and warned that discrimination would prevent him from succeeding in industry. But Wang remained confident and set out to prove them wrong. "I thought: 'Maybe I can be in business for myself one year. I'm a Ph.D. I believe in computers. I am a computer expert.' So I gambled on myself. I decided to be self-employed," he stated. "A lot of this was confidence. I actually believed I could succeed. Confidence, you know, is nothing more than facing a problem and believing you can overcome it. I have always believed I could overcome the odds."

In the early days of his business, Wang sold memory cores and designed a variety of commercial applications for them, such as electronic controls for production machinery. He also worked under contract with other companies to do special technology projects. One of his first successes was creating an electronic scoreboard for New York's Shea Stadium. He later helped another company develop a revolutionary system called LINASEC that set newspaper type in even columns. "I used to get a lot of ideas while driving home from work," Wang recalled. "This is one reason that my associates finally prevailed on me to accept a chauffeur. They were afraid that I would get so caught up in thinking about a problem that I might not pay attention to an oncoming truck, and they felt it would be better for both me and Wang Laboratories if I did not drive while thinking about work."

Over time, Wang Laboratories gradually expanded and added employees. Wang moved his operations to larger offices in 1954 and several times afterward, eventually building a headquarters in the Boston suburb of Lowell, Massachusetts. In June 1955, Wang Laboratories became a corporation, and Wang became its president. The following year, Wang entered negotiations with International Business Machines (IBM) — which was in the process of becoming a leading computer company — for the sale of his memory core patent. It turned out to be a difficult situation for Wang due to IBM's huge size, complicated decision-making processes, and rough negotiating tactics. Although he did not get the million dollars he asked for, he did receive $400,000 for the patent — a significant sum at a time when his annual income was $10,000. He also learned several things from the experience that would help him to compete with IBM later.

The Remarkable Growth of Wang Laboratories

The sale of the memory core patent allowed Wang to expand his business. He decided to focus on making people's jobs easier by introducing electronic equipment into the workplace. The first major breakthrough for Wang Laboratories came in 1965 with the invention of the LOCI (logarithmic calculating instrument) desktop calculator. This machine could add, subtract, multiply, compute square roots, and perform a variety of other mathematical calculations that scientists and engineers needed in their work. Before this time, scientists and engineers had to use manual instruments called slide rules or enormous mainframe computers to help them with complex equations. Only large companies and scientific institutions could afford computers — which were very large and expensive — and they were used almost exclusively for mathematical calculations. This stands in contrast to the situation today, when many people have small desktop and laptop computers in their homes that can be used for a wide variety of purposes, and small calculators that cost under $10 can perform many of the functions that used to take large computers.

Dr. An Wang at Wang Laboratories, September 15, 1969

Since Wang's LOCI was faster and more advanced than competing calculator models, he was awarded a patent on his invention. Although each LOCI system sold for $6,500, this was still considerably cheaper than a mainframe computer. In 1966, Wang introduced the LOCI Model 300, which was cheaper and easier to use than the original, and sales skyrocketed. By 1967, Wang Laboratories had expanded into a million-dollar business that employed 400 people. When Wang sold stock in his company to the public that year, it was very popular among investors. In fact, the price increased from $12 to $37 per share on the first day of trading, making Wang a very rich man.

Before long, Wang Laboratories earned a reputation for being able to predict what consumers wanted. As Wang explained, he and his company could often "find a need and fill it." This remarkable foresight helped the company continue to grow rapidly over the next few years. By 1970, it reached $25 million in sales and had 1,500 employees. The next major breakthrough for Wang Laboratories came in 1971, with the invention of the first word processor. Before this time, people used cumbersome manual typewriters to prepare business documents. The Wang word processor made typing jobs much easier by offering functions to proofread and correct the text of typed documents before printing a final copy. Even though the earliest word processors only let users review a few lines of text at a time, they still increased office productivity dramatically.

> *"People say I'm successful. I've achieved a lot. But every time you accomplish a goal, there's still another goal. Success is not an end unto itself. It's insatiable, something without an end. Every time I succeed at something, I can see so much more to conquer."*

Wang's decision to move his business away from calculators and into word processors was somewhat controversial. Many investors thought that the company could continue to grow and earn money by producing calculators. But Wang recognized that, with the invention of microchip technology, calculators would continue to become smaller and less expensive. He felt that his company could not continue to compete in the calculator market unless they began to manufacture chips. At this point, he reorganized the stock of his company in order to give his family greater control over such decisions. "We want to concentrate on building our company," he said at the time. "We do not want to be distracted by fighting takeovers and that sort of thing."

In 1976, Wang introduced a new and improved word processing system called the WPS. The WPS displayed the entire text of a typed document on a large, television-like screen. It also provided users with a simple series of menus that allowed them to move whole words or sentences around. This invention was so revolutionary that when marketing personnel from Wang Laboratories first demonstrated it at a trade show, people lined up 10 deep to watch. The WPS sold extremely well and transformed Wang Laboratories from a calculator company into a word processing company.

By the late 1970s, Wang's company had posted a remarkable string of 26 straight quarters of record growth. In fact, Wang Laboratories grew at an impressive average annual rate of 42 percent from its inception in 1951 through the early 1980s. Most of its nearly 20,000 employees also found it a rewarding place to work. Wang provided his people with generous benefits — including some of the earliest on-site day-care centers and fitness facilities in industry — and a supportive working environment. But just when it appeared as if everything Wang did would turn out right, his business took a downturn.

The Decline of Wang Laboratories

Beginning in the early 1980s, Wang Laboratories ran into a long series of problems. Wang wanted to expand his company's business to include complete office automation systems, integrating a number of different computer technologies into the workplace. But in this emerging field, he had to compete directly against much larger competitors, including IBM, AT&T, and Hewlett-Packard. In addition, Wang was slow to recognize that IBM had become the standard format for office systems. Since Wang products were not compatible with IBM systems, they did not sell well.

The company's rapid growth had caused some internal problems as well. Communication within the company was poor, resulting in disorganized and inefficient ways of doing business. "Since we are growing so fast, our organization is weaker than it should be," Wang admitted. "Paperwork procedures and systems are always behind." Wang Laboratories was also criticized for announcing the development of revolutionary new products, then either not being able to deliver on orders or delivering products that did not perform well. "We were too aggressive. Research and development couldn't keep up the pace," Wang explained.

In 1981, Wang gave up some of his control of the company. Instead of leading on his own, he formed a management committee that included his son Frederick and marketing expert John F. Cunningham. Two years later, Wang named Cunningham president of the company. Unfortunately, Wang Laboratories' financial problems continued. When earnings dropped from $210 million in 1984 to $15 million in 1985, Cunningham resigned and Wang again took over control of the company. "As long as I am having fun, I will be both president and chairman for the next few years," he said at the time. In an attempt to turn things around, he laid off 1,600 workers and instituted cost-cut-

Dr. An Wang with wife, Lorraine, at their home in Lincoln, MA, 1983

ting measures. He also personally visited more than 50 sales offices around the country and the world to get a better understanding of what customers wanted. In 1986, Wang Laboratories landed a $480 million contract to sell minicomputers to the U.S. Air Force, which helped raise earnings to $56 million that year.

At the end of 1986, Wang named his son Frederick president of the company. This move had long been expected, as Chinese tradition dictates that fathers pass the family business down to their eldest sons. But Frederick Wang, who was then 37 years old, was not as well liked within the company as his father. Some people resented his short temper, while others simply did not believe he could fill his father's shoes. Wang Laboratories soon announced a series of new products, including voice-controlled computers and visual scanning technology that could read and store paper forms like an electronic filing cabinet. But the company still had trouble finding the right products for a rapidly changing marketplace, and it also struggled against an overall slump in the computer business. As a result, Wang Laboratories posted a $71 million loss in 1987.

As the company's financial situation continued to worsen, An Wang began to experience serious health problems. Doctors discovered a cancerous tumor in his throat in March 1989. He was treated with chemotherapy for several months, and then had surgery to remove the tumor in July. When Wang

Laboratories lost $424 million in 1989, even after laying off 2,400 workers, the ailing Wang removed his son from the presidency and replaced him with Richard Miller, an executive from outside the company. Although this decision was very difficult for Wang, the move was necessary to reassure the company's creditors and investors.

Founder's Death Seals Company's Fate

Sadly, An Wang died of cancer of the esophagus on March 24, 1990, at the age of 70. Memorial services held at Harvard University were attended by Massachusetts Governor Michael Dukakis as well as 300 other dignitaries and friends. Additional services held at the Wang Laboratories headquarters in Lowell attracted over 2,000 mourners. Wang was beloved by his employees, who referred to him as "the Doctor" in recognition of his academic degrees. Wang was one of the richest men in the United States, with wealth estimated at $1.6 billion in the mid-1980s. He built the largest minority-owned company in the United States with his visionary business sense. His development of the calculator, word processor, and early office automation systems revolutionized the way that work was performed in offices around the country. He also held 40 patents on inventions that were vital to computer science. Despite all his achievements, however, Wang still lived a quiet, simple life in accordance with his Confucian philosophy. In fact, he only owned two business suits at any one time.

"When young people ask me how to succeed, I always tell them to work harder than they intended. People have to exert extra effort, to go the extra mile. There is a success attitude. It's positive. You have to say to yourself, 'I'm going to make it.'"

Shortly before his death, Wang published a book called *Lessons* in which he shared some of the personal beliefs that contributed to his success. "People say I'm successful. I've achieved a lot. But every time you accomplish a goal, there's still another goal. Success is not an end unto itself. It's insatiable, something without an end. Every time I succeed at something, I can see so much more to conquer," he wrote. "When young people ask me how to succeed, I always tell them to work harder than they intended. People have to exert extra effort, to go the extra mile. There is a success attitude. It's positive. You have to say to yourself, 'I'm going to make it.' It's important to be psychologically comfortable. I've always tried to put myself in the right frame of mind."

Wang Laboratories continued to decline after its founder's death. The Wang family sold off much of its interest, and the company filed for bankruptcy in August 1992. Although Wang Laboratories emerged from bankruptcy and still exists today, it has changed dramatically. It is led by an all new management team, and it now makes computer software instead of hardware.

MARRIAGE AND FAMILY

Wang married Lorraine Chiu on July 10, 1949. The couple met in Boston at a social gathering of Chinese students and professionals when he was working as a research assistant at Harvard and she was a graduate student in English at nearby Wellesley College. Lorraine was originally from Shanghai, like An, but they had never met there. The Wangs had three children: sons Frederick and Courtney, and daughter Juliette. Until his death, Wang lived in a 10-room house on 20 acres of property in Lincoln, Massachusetts.

HOBBIES AND OTHER INTERESTS

Wang's main hobby was tennis, which he played every Tuesday with his son Frederick or with other executives from Wang Laboratories. In addition to his success as a businessman, Wang was known for his many charitable contributions to the Boston community. In accordance with his Confucian philosophy, he believed that serving the community was very important. "It's not just an act by one individual," he commented. "It's an attempt to create a spirit of awareness in which everyone can participate."

In 1983, Wang donated $4 million to restore Boston's performing arts theater, which was renamed the Wang Center for Performing Arts. He also provided the funding for an outpatient clinic at Massachusetts General Hospital. Wang believed in helping people less fortunate than himself. This belief inspired him to donate a computer network to New York City's center for the homeless, and to construct a $15 million assembly plant in Boston's impoverished Chinatown neighborhood to provide jobs to local residents. When he was unable to find the types of employees he wanted at Wang Laboratories, Wang spent $6 million to create an independent, nonprofit school, the Wang Institute of Graduate Studies. The Wang Institute educates students in both computer science and business management. "I want to give back something to the community that has given me so much," he explained.

WRITINGS

Lessons: An Autobiography, 1986 (with Eugene Linden)

HONORS AND AWARDS

Medal of Achievement (American Electronics Association): 1984
U.S. Medal of Liberty: 1986
DATAMATION Hall of Fame: 1987
U.S. National Inventors Hall of Fame: 1988

FURTHER READING

Books

Annual Obituary 1990

Contemporary Authors, Vol. 132

Encyclopedia Britannica, 1995

Encyclopedia of World Biography, 1987

Grolier Library of North American Biographies: Entrepreneurs and Inventors, Vol. 3, 1994

Ingham, John N. *Contemporary American Business Leaders: A Biographical Dictionary*, 1990

Hargrove, Jim. *Dr. An Wang: Computer Pioneer*, 1993 (juvenile)

Kenney, Charles. *Riding the Runaway Horse: The Rise and Decline of Wang Laboratories*, 1992

Mavis, Barbara. *Contemporary American Success Stories: Famous People of Asian Ancestry*, 1994 (juvenile)

Morey, Janet Nomura, and Wendy Dunn. *Famous Asian Americans*, 1992 (juvenile)

Notable Asian Americans, 1995

Wang, An, with Eugene Linden. *Lessons: An Autobiography*, 1986

Who Was Who in America, 1989-93

Periodicals

Boston Globe, Nov. 26, 1989, Metro section, p.1; Nov. 27, 1989, Business section, p.1

Business Month, Feb. 1990, p.22

Business Week, Nov. 13, 1971, p.102; May 17, 1982, p.100; Apr. 18, 1986, p.222; June 30, 1986, p.78

Current Biography Yearbook 1987; 1990 (obituary)

Financial World, Sep. 15, 1981, p.27

Forbes, Oct. 15, 1976; Sep. 29, 1980, p.149; Feb. 15, 1982, p.36

Fortune, Feb 3, 1986, p.106

Industry Week, Oct. 13, 1986, p.55

New York Times, Feb. 24, 1980, p.C3; May 5, 1984, p.A1; Mar. 25, 1990, p.38

New York Times Biographical Service, Mar. 1990, p.290

Time, Nov. 17, 1980, p.81

Wall Street Journal, Nov. 6, 1984, p.22

Washington Post, Mar. 25, 1990, p.D4

Photo and Illustration Credits

Jane Brody/Photos: Michael Howard; AP/Wide World Photos.

Seymour Cray/Photos: Courtesy of city of Chippewa Falls Cray Supercomputer Collection.

Paul Erdös/Photos: Photos from the documentary film *N is a Number: A Portrait of Paul Erdös*, © 1993 by George Paul Csicsery.

Walter Gilbert/Photos: Harvard University/Office of News and Public Affairs; UPI/Corbis-Bettmann.

Stephen Jay Gould/Photos: Rhonda Roland Shearer; Steven Liss/TIME magazine. Covers: WONDERFUL LIFE copyright © 1989 by Stephen Jay Gould. Cover design by Mike McIver. Cover painting by Charles Knight, courtesy National Geographic Society; DINOSAUR IN A HAYSTACK copyright © 1995 Crown Publishers.

Shirley Ann Jackson/Photo: AP/Wide World Photos.

Raymond Kurzweil/Photos: UPI/Corbis-Bettmann.

Shannon Lucid/Photos: NASA

Margaret Mead/Photos: UPI/Corbis-Bettmann.

Garrett Morgan/Photos: Courtesy of the Western Reserve Historical Society.

Bill Nye/Photos: Copyright © Buena Vista Television; Copyright © 1993 Walt Disney Company; Copyright © Buena Vista Television; Copyright © 1993 Walt Disney Company.

Eloy Rodriguez/Photos: Frank DiMeo/Cornell University Photography; David Lynch-Benjamin/Cornell University Photography.

An Wang/Photos: All Boston Globe Staff Photos/Frank O'Brien; Jim Wilson; Phillip Preston.

Guide to the Indexes

Each volume of *Biography Today* contains four indexes: Name Index, General Index, Places of Birth Index, and Birthday Index. Each index is fully cumulative, covering the regular series of *Biography Today* as well as the special subject volumes.

The **Regular Series** of *Biography Today* is denoted in the indexes with the month and year of the issue in which the individual appeared. Each individual also appears in the cumulation for that year.

Albright, Madeleine	Apr 97
Dion, Celine	Sep 97
Ford, Harrison	Sep 97
Jordan, Barbara	Apr 96
Reeve, Christopher	Jan 97
Robinson, David	Sep 96
White, Jaleel	Jan 96

The **Special Subject Volumes** of *Biography Today* are each denoted in the indexes with an abbreviated form of the series name, plus the year of that volume. They are listed as follows:

Adams, Ansel	Artist 96	(Artists Series)
Dahl, Roald	Author 95	(Authors Series)
Gibbs, Lois	Env 97	(World Leaders Series: Environmental Leaders
Mandela, Winnie	ModAfr 97	(World Leaders Series: Modern African Leaders
Sagan, Carl	Science 96	(Scientists & Inventors Series)
Woods, Tiger	Sport 96	(Sports Series)

Updated information on certain individuals appears in the **Appendix** at the end of the *Biography Today* Annual Cumulation. In the indexes, the original entry is listed first, followed by any updates:

Gore, Al	Jan 93; Update 96; Update 97
Myers, Walter Dean	Jan 93; Update 94

Name Index

Listed below are the names of all individuals profiled in *Biography Today,* followed by the date of the issue in which they appear.

General Index

This index includes subjects, occupations, organizations, and ethnic and minority origins that pertain to individuals profiled in *Biography Today*.

First Lady of the United States

football coaches

football players

foster children

French

"Fresh Prince of Bel-Air"

Friends of the Earth

"Full House"

Garfield

general, U.S. Army

genetics

Places of Birth Index

The following index lists the places of birth for the individuals profiled in *Biography Today*. Places of birth are entered under state, province, and/or country.

Birthday Index

People to Appear in Future Issues

Actors
Trini Alvarado
Richard Dean
　Anderson
Dan Aykroyd
Tyra Banks
Drew Barrymore
Levar Burton
Cher
Kevin Costner
Courtney Cox
Tom Cruise
Jamie Lee Curtis
Patti D'Arbanville-
　Quinn
Geena Davis
Ozzie Davis
Ruby Dee
Michael De Lorenzo
Matt Dillon
Michael Douglas
Larry Fishburne
Jody Foster
Morgan Freeman
Richard Gere
Tracey Gold
Graham Greene
Mark Harmon
Michael Keaton
Val Kilmer
Angela Lansbury
Joey Lawrence
Martin Lawrence
Christopher Lloyd
Kellie Martin
Marlee Matlin
Bette Midler
Alyssa Milano
Demi Moore
Rick Moranis
Tamera Mowry
Tia Mowry
Kate Mulgrew
Eddie Murphy
Liam Neeson
Leonard Nimoy
Sean Penn
Phylicia Rashad
Keanu Reeves
Jason James Richter

Julia Roberts
Bob Saget
Arnold
　Schwarzenegger
Alicia Silverstone
Christian Slater
Taran Noah Smith
Jimmy Smits
Wesley Snipes
Sylvester Stallone
John Travolta
Mario Van Peebles
Damon Wayans
Sigourney Weaver
Bruce Willis
B.D. Wong
Malik Yoba

Artists
Mitsumasa Anno
Graeme Base
Yoko Ono

Astronauts
Neil Armstrong

Authors
Jean M. Auel
John Christopher
Arthur C. Clarke
John Colville
Paula Danziger
Paula Fox
Jamie Gilson
Rosa Guy
Nat Hentoff
Norma Klein
Lois Lowry
Stephen Manes
Norma Fox Mazer
Anne McCaffrey
Gloria D. Miklowitz
Marsha Norman
Robert O'Brien
Francine Pascal
Daniel Pinkwater
Louis Sachar
John Saul
Amy Tan

Alice Walker
Jane Yolen
Roger Zelazny

Business
Minoru Arakawa
Michael Eisner
David Geffen
Wayne Huizenga
Donna Karan
Phil Knight
Estee Lauder
Sheri Poe
Anita Roddick
Donald Trump
Ted Turner
Lillian Vernon

Cartoonists
Lynda Barry
Roz Chast
Greg Evans
Nicole Hollander
Art Spiegelman
Garry Trudeau

Comedians
Billy Crystal
Steve Martin
Eddie Murphy
Bill Murray
Chris Rock

Dancers
Debbie Allen
Mikhail Baryshnikov
Sanon Glover
Gregory Hines
Twyla Tharp
Tommy Tune

Directors/Producers
Woody Allen
Steven Bocho
Tim Burton
Francis Ford Coppola
Ron Howard
John Hughes
Penny Marshall
Leonard Nimoy

Rob Reiner
John Singleton
Quentin Tarantino

**Environmentalists/
Animal Rights**
Kathryn Fuller
Linda Maraniss
Ingrid Newkirk
Pat Potter

Journalists
Tom Brokaw
John Hockenberry
Ted Koppel
Jim Lehrer
Dan Rather
Nina Totenberg
Mike Wallace
Bob Woodward

Musicians
Ace of Base
Aqua
Babyface
Basia
George Benson
Bjork
Clint Black
Ruben Blades
Mary J. Blige
Bono
Edie Brickell
James Brown
Ray Charles
Chayanne
Natalie Cole
Sean "Puffy" Combs
Cowboy Junkies
Sheryl Crow
Billy Ray Cyrus
Melissa Etheridge
Aretha Franklin
Green Day
Guns N' Roses
P.J. Harvey
Hootie & the Blowfish
India
Janet Jackson
Michael Jackson
Jewel

Winona Judd
R. Kelly
Anthony Kiedis
Lenny Kravitz
Kris Kross
James Levine
LL Cool J
Andrew Lloyd Webber
Courtney Love
Lyle Lovett
MC Lyte
Madonna
Barbara Mandrell
Branford Marsalis
Paul McCartney
Midori
Morrissey
N.W.A.
Jesseye Norman
Sinead O'Connor
Luciano Pavoratti
Pearl Jam
Teddy Pendergrass
David Pirner
Prince
Public Enemy
Raffi
Bonnie Raitt
Red Hot Chili Peppers
Lou Reed
L.A. Reid
R.E.M.
Trent Reznor
Kenny Rogers
Axl Rose
Run-D.M.C.
Paul Simon
Smashing Pumpkins
Sting
Michael Stipe
Pam Tillis
TLC
Randy Travis
Terence Trent d'Arby

Travis Tritt
Shania Twain
U2
Eddie Vedder
Stevie Wonder
Trisha Yearwood
Dwight Yoakum
Neil Young

Politics/World Leaders
Harry A. Blackmun
Jesse Brown
Pat Buchanan
Mangosuthu Buthelezi
Violeta Barrios de
  Chamorro
Shirley Chisolm
Jean Chretien
Warren Christopher
Edith Cresson
Mario Cuomo
Dalai Lama
Mike Espy
Alan Greenspan
Vaclav Havel
Jack Kemp
Bob Kerrey
Kim Il-Sung
Coretta Scott King
John Major
Imelda Marcos
Slobodan Milosevic
Mother Teresa
Ralph Nader
Manuel Noriega
Hazel O'Leary
Leon Panetta
Federico Pena
Simon Peres
Robert Reich
Ann Richards
Richard Riley

Phyllis Schlafly
Donna Shalala
Desmond Tutu
Lech Walesa
Eli Weisel
Vladimir Zhirinovsky

Royalty
Charles, Prince of
  Wales
Duchess of York (Sarah
  Ferguson)
Queen Noor

Scientists
Sallie Baliunas
Avis Cohen
Donna Cox
Mimi Koehl
Deborah Letourneau
Philippa Marrack
Helen Quinn
Barbara Smuts
Flossie Wong-Staal
Aslihan Yener
Adrienne Zihlman

Sports
Jim Abbott
Michael Andretti
Boris Becker
Barry Bonds
Bobby Bonilla
Jose Canseco
Jennifer Capriati
Michael Chang
Roger Clemens
Randall Cunningham
Eric Davis
Clyde Drexler
George Foreman
Zina Garrison
Rickey Henderson
Evander Holyfield

Brett Hull
Raghib Ismail
Jim Kelly
Petr Klima
Willy Mays
Paul Molitor
Joe Paterno
Kirby Puckett
Pat Riley
Mark Rippien
Daryl Strawberry
Danny Sullivan
Vinnie Testaverde
Isiah Thomas
Mike Tyson

Television Personalities
Andre Brown
  (Dr. Dre)
Katie Couric
Phil Donahue
Kathie Lee Gifford
Ed Gordon
Arsenio Hall
Ricki Lake
Joan Lunden
Dennis Miller
Diane Sawyer
Alison Stewart
Jon Stewart
Vanna White
Montel Williams
Paul Zaloom

Other
James Brady
Johnnetta Cole
David Copperfield
Jaimie Escalante
Jack Kevorkian
Wendy Kopp
Sister Irene Kraus
Jeanne White